ESSENTIAL HEALING

Hypnotherapy and Regression-Based Practices to Release the Emotional Pain and Trauma Keeping You Stuck

PAUL AURAND

REVEAL PRESS

AN IMPRINT OF NEW HARBINGER PUBLICATIONS

Publisher's Note

Distributed in Canada by Raincoast Books

Copyright © 2021 by Paul Aurand
                  Reveal Press
                  An imprint of New Harbinger Publications, Inc.
                  5674 Shattuck Avenue
                  Oakland, CA 94609
                  www.newharbinger.com

Life Between Lives® and LBL® are registered trademarks of the Michael Newton Institute for Life Between Lives Hypnotherapy. http://www.newtoninstitute.org

Cover design by Amy Shoup

Acquired by Ryan Buresh

Edited by Gretel Hakanson

All Rights Reserved

Library of Congress Cataloging-in-Publication Data

Names: Aurand, Paul, author. | Alexander, Eben, author.
Title: Essential healing : hypnotherapy and regression-based practices to release the emotional pain and trauma keeping you stuck / Paul Aurand, Eben Alexander.
Description: Oakland, CA : New Harbinger Publications, [2021] | Includes bibliographical references.
Identifiers: LCCN 2020052590 | ISBN 9781684036806 (trade paperback)
Subjects: LCSH: Post-traumatic stress disorder--Treatment. | Psychic trauma--Treatment. | Hypnotism--Therapeutic use.
Classification: LCC RC552.P67 A95 2021 | DDC 616.85/2106--dc23
LC record available at https://lccn.loc.gov/2020052590

Printed in the United States of America

23   22   21

10   9   8   7   6   5   4   3   2   1   First Printing

Contents

Foreword

Over the last few decades, progress in psychology, neuroscience, and philosophy of mind has been converging on evidence of the true existence of the soul, as a higher sense of the self, in its life journey. Even modern medicine acknowledges that our beliefs about treatment can strongly influence our health by using the placebo effect to evaluate any new treatment. The healing power of the mind, demonstrated by the placebo effect, is undeniable amidst extraordinary examples of spontaneous remission of advanced cancers, infections that go away beyond any explanation from conventional medicine, and miraculous healing during near-death experiences. These all illuminate the power our will can have in manifesting improved health. Modern medicine fully acknowledges the role our attitudes play in influencing our physical health, which makes it clear that our consciousness and beliefs have at least as much effect in healing our psyches and, ultimately, our souls. It is high time we allowed the power of belief to flourish in all realms of overall health.

The marvelous book you are holding represents the power of having an experienced hypnotherapist, who has had a profound near-death experience that helped guide his craft, share his shift in world view and his personal and professional practice in ways that will greatly benefit people in need of healing.

Beginning with his near-death experience after being struck by lightning two decades ago, and the profound personal lessons it engendered over time, Paul carefully guides the reader through progressively refined layers of interaction with deeper aspects of themselves, all while clarifying various options for learning and teaching along the path. The first step is realizing we are not our "ego mind," or that running stream of thoughts in our head. The solution is to access that "door to our inner world"—the heart. This is where so much of the trauma from our child-hood, and even earlier, serves as baggage that needs to be processed and ultimately assimilated. The book includes numerous specific and illus-trative clinical cases to help paint a clear picture of the problems encoun-tered and their eventual resolution through this powerful therapeutic program. In addition, Paul has included very specific exercises to help the reader as if he were right there, guiding them through the process.

Access to the heart facilitates recognition and release of various emotions that might have hindered our growth, as well as the processing of related beliefs (about self and the world) and survival strategies that might indicate a suboptimal relationship with the world at large. Engaging the heart ultimately allows access to both the wounded child and the wonder child within us all. Identification of various parts of self allows for their integration into a whole, a crucial step in working toward knowledge and healing of the soul. Refinement of this process involves further disentanglement of various aspects of self and progressive inte-gration into a more wholistic identity.

In these more advanced layers of work, Paul helps the reader recog-nize and communicate with their guides residing in the spiritual realm and come to see the great wisdom that lies within. As the modern neu-roscientific notion of the one mind we all share, that primordial con-sciousness at the heart of all being, comes into better focus, we realize the benefits such a powerful world view offers to support the reality of this exceptional soul work. As final steps, Paul incorporates life reviews (modeled after their common occurrence in many of the most powerful and transformative near-death experiences) and much of the wisdom from his role guiding the Michael Newton Institute, with a rich reper-toire of hypnotic regressions not only to recover soul memories from past lives, but also the crucial work that Newton introduced around Life-Between-Lives hypnotic regression. The ultimate layer in this effective program involves connecting with your soul essence.

Be prepared for gems of knowledge, illuminating insights, and anecdotes that make this book relevant to a wide range of soul journey issues. The clinical examples greatly enrich and simplify the book's overall utility and applicability to the individual seeker. It has much to offer other clinicians interested in pursuing this essential soul work, but is written in an engaging, heartfelt, and personal style that will appeal to a wide range of readers, from beginner to advanced.

So, bon voyage on your exploration of discovering your soul's very reason for existence and of identification and alignment with your soul essence!

> —Eben Alexander, MD, neurosurgeon and author of
> *Proof of Heaven, The Map of Heaven,* and *Living in a Mindful Universe*

Struck by an En-Lightning Experience

On the day I turned forty, I was sitting on a beach meditating when I had a spontaneous inner experience of diving into myself and passing through all the layers that I thought of as me. These layers comprised my mental or rational mind, my feeling heart, many stored emotions, my inner child, and other parts of my psyche that had served me through life. After a while, I came upon a little flame, like the pilot light on a stove, and it gradually grew into a more substantial glow, almost like a bonfire that beckoned me into it. As I answered the call, the fire seemed to burn through all those crusty layers that had accumulated over the years— and, from my perspective, over past lifetimes as well. The layers contained deposits of shielding, of fabricated stories that were intended to protect me from the hurts, wounds, and disappointments of life, but that now separated me from the core of my being, something that I came to call my "soul essence."

We all have accumulated these encrusted layers of hurt from early life and from the defenses we've created to prevent further hurt, which have accumulated and covered our deep inner spirit over time. These layers obscure what is a magnificent you, your own authentic soul essence. It is the divine spark within you that is wise far beyond intellect, that emanates unconditional love, and is one with all things. It is also the part of you that will continue to exist after your physical body and brain have died. Some people call it nonlocal consciousness or simply the soul. The name isn't important as long as you learn to recognize its presence within you. Some Eastern traditions speak of this inner nature as being obscured from us much as the sun can be hidden from sight on a cloudy day. The sun is always there, of course; we just have to find a way to get through the clouds.

As I sat on the beach that day, the dancing, illuminated feeling of breaking through my layers of inner protection represented a kind of expanded consciousness that I had tried to achieve by meditation for years without much success. That feeling, which stayed with me for several days, was not the same as my soul essence, but it allowed me to feel its presence inside of me with all the warmth and brightness of a hundred suns.

I wouldn't say that I'm able to maintain that blissful, expanded state on a regular basis, but with careful tending—the kind I share in this book—it's much more alive within me now. When I take people on the journey to reconnect with their soul essence, they run into the same obstructive layers I experienced on that beach, including several block-ages that keep us stuck and prevent or limit our ability to make contact with the rich inner layers of intuitive wisdom, soul memories, and soul essence at our innermost core. Essential Healing is a process that will help you get in touch with your soul essence and become whole again, with body, mind, and spirit connected and working in unison. I developed my Essential Healing practice as a way to work through the layers that I've described, addressing them in sequence as I will do throughout the nine chapters of this book, devoting a chapter to each of the nine layers: mental mind, feeling heart, stored emotions, your inner child, archetypal aspects and parts of the psyche, parental and ancestral baggage, inner wisdom, soul memory, and soul essence.

While we can long for awakening experiences like the one I had on my fortieth birthday, which are blissful, we need to be aware that they also often come through intense pain. We have all been through some form of traumatic event, most likely many of them, and we survived them to the best of our abilities in the moment. But what happens afterward determines whether this pain closes us down or whether we see it as an invitation to heal, open, and receive gifts from our soul essence so we can live from the core of unconditional love and wisdom that we sense is there.

The Shock That Charged My Soul Essence

We can read about unconditional love all we want, even long for it, but how often do we experience it in our lives? Parents may feel unconditional love for a newborn, but even that will be tested as the child grows up. Unconditional love isn't based on pleasing anyone, learning anything, how we look, or how smart or athletic or even how compassionate we are. Our intuition tells us that deep within each of us lives a great spirit of profound wisdom, creativity, and power, with the ability to give and receive unconditional love. I considered myself capable of romantic love, the love of a child for my parents, and the love of a parent for my own child. But I had never felt unconditional love until I was struck by lightning. To be clear, the unconditional love I am speaking about, which is also described by people who have had near-death experiences as well as by countless mystics, is a love beyond any human love. It is a totally accepting, all-embracing love that fills you completely to your core. When I later re-engaged my experience of being struck by lightning through a powerful form of hypnosis, the effects of that shock moved into my conscious mind to profoundly change the course of my life.

Four years after my initial awakening on the beach, in the summer of 1998, I took my three-year-old son, Orion, to a swim meet at Greenwood Lake, a narrow, seven-mile-long body of water that straddles the border between upstate New York and New Jersey. It was a gloriously sunny day in June, and I could hardly think of a lovelier place to be, a glistening lake surrounded by lush state forest. The only drag on my enthusiasm was that the lifeguards had postponed the start of the meet to allow a thunderstorm just north of the lake to pass. I thought they were being cautious to a fault because, while we could hear far-off rumbles of thunder, I didn't see the sky darkening, even in the distance. After waiting some time, the lifeguards announced that we'd have to wait even longer because the storm hadn't moved on. I settled back in my beach chair and pulled a cold drink out of the cooler. But my three-year-old was having a harder time relaxing. Bored and antsy, Orion wanted to leave. I had to admit it wasn't much fun sitting around, not allowed even to dip a toe in the lake because of concerns about possible lightning strikes.

Orion became more insistent. "Go home, Daddy," he cried. "Go home!" Just a few moments later when the lifeguards announced that the meet was delayed again, I decided to leave. Gathering the beach chairs and coolers, we walked up the hill to where the car was parked near a storm drain. After securing Orion in the front seat, I loaded the beach stuff in the trunk and got out my keys. In the next moment, I both heard and felt an explosion, as if a bomb had gone off, accompanied by a searing flash of white light. The impact of the explosion shook me to the core. I had no idea exactly what was happening. I had seen some power lines and a transformer overhead, and I thought maybe the transformer had shorted out, but the noise was way too loud for that. It was—*deafening!*

But along with the ear-splitting sound, a rattling vibration shook my entire body. Completely rigid now, I shuddered so emphatically that I was bouncing up and down on the pavement. The baseball cap I was wearing popped straight up off my head, and my glasses flew off my face as if in a scene in an animated cartoon. At least, that's what the people standing nearby later told me. They also said they witnessed tentacles of lightning emerge from the storm drain that I was standing near and leap onto me. The bolt burned right up my legs, arced between my chest and left arm, went out my arm, and blew the keys out of my hand where I stood behind the trunk. From there it jumped straight into the car, frying the electrical system, emerged from the front of the car, and knocked down another person standing there. Because Orion was safely in the front seat, he wasn't harmed.

But I was ignorant of all those details. As electricity roared through me, I felt like I was fighting for my life. The pain was excruciating, like getting thousands of charley horses all at once. I instinctively raged against the relentless charge of energy invading me. "*No!*" I screamed in my mind. "*Get out of my body!*"

A lightning bolt can course through a human body in just three milliseconds, and it does most of its damage to the head, shoulders, and upper torso. Besides sending upward of 150 million volts of electrical power through me, the strike heated the surrounding air to 50,000 degrees Fahrenheit, which left feather burns—a distinctive pattern caused by the moisture on my legs—and blistering on my arm and torso. "The jolt from lightning typically follows the nervous system," Dr. Michael Murano, a surgeon at the burn unit of St. Barnabas Medical Center in Livingston, New York, was quoted as saying in a newspaper account the next day. "The nerves conduct best. That's their specialized function, to conduct electricity."[1] My nerves were clearly doing their job.

Despite the extremely short duration of the strike, for me time slowed down as the aftershocks continued to rock my body. I had enough time to think that I was wearing rubber-soled sandals and I should be insulated, although obviously I wasn't. In fact, just then I flew through the air, like a missile being launched in an arc, and slammed back to the ground about six feet away, landing on my head. At that point, my conscious memory seemed to go blank. When the lightning struck me, rain hadn't yet started to fall. By the time I became aware again, I was lying in several inches of water, and rain and hail and wind were raging all around me. I still can't say how long I was out, but it must have taken at least ten or fifteen minutes for the storm to materialize so fully.

Ninety percent of lightning strike victims do survive, although usually with significant injuries.[2] Witnesses told me that the lightning initially struck a big tree near the car, traveled into the storm drain, and came back out before it walloped into me. That roundabout route may have saved my life because it's rare to escape a direct hit without severe injury, including brain damage (the cellular structure of your brain is cooked by the current). The result can be short-term memory loss or amnesia, temporary or permanent paralysis, seizures, blown eardrums, cataracts, and chronic pain.

As I lay stunned and roiling in agony on the ground in a kind of delirium, the other parents stood back, discussing the potential danger of touching someone who has been struck by lightning—a myth. The storm had knocked down a lot of trees, blocking the main roads, so it took some time for the police and ambulance to arrive. The police got there first and carried me and Orion into a nearby car because the rain and hail were heavy. We waited nearly an hour for the ambulance to come, only to realize they'd forgotten to bring their defibrillator. Fortunately, we didn't need one. Doctors at the hospital did their best to relieve the pain and trauma I was suffering, as well as the burns, but the hospital had virtually no experience with survivors of lightning strikes. While I was there, I behaved erratically, alternating between sobbing and laughing, cracking morbid jokes, and thanking a God in whom I didn't really believe. At one point I pulled a blanket over my shoulders like a superhero cape and walked around the hospital shouting that I was the Savior.

In the days that followed, I discovered that some of the aftereffects of the strike were not so easily treated. I had persistent back pain. I was hypersensitive not only to storms but also to electricity in its many forms. I was sometimes afraid to open the refrigerator door or to turn on a lamp. Hours before a storm arrived, I could feel it in my legs, which started to hurt like they did the day after the lightning hit. My energy level was frustratingly low, and the memory loss frightening.

I struggled to get back to normal, while unsure exactly what normal meant. What did I want my life to be? Would I make the most of this bizarre experience, or would I allow it to hobble me for the rest of my existence? A few friends and colleagues said I had been touched by God. But others opined that devils were after me. Some called it a shamanic initiation, but during my struggle to recover and then continue with my life, I didn't feel there was anything sacred about it. It wasn't until I entered a deep form of the hypnotic state I had long been using to help others heal that I realized just how powerful hypnosis can be for spiritual awakening.

What Hypnotherapy Really Does

I'll pause my story to clarify what hypnosis is and share the ways my use of it as a therapeutic treatment have evolved. You have probably seen a staged demonstration of hypnosis—if not in person at a club, then most likely in films or on television—in which the stage hypnotist enlists a few volunteers from the audience. I've observed several such sessions and took part in one, and my experience was instructive. The stage hypnotist generally finds a way to determine which audience members are the most responsive to suggestion. In a disguised way, he makes suggestions that the members who come on stage are going to have fun and enjoy being part of the show. "Who wants to come up," he'll say, "and really have a good time?" And once you go up there, with a few hundred people watching you, you may feel more foolish *not* doing the silly things he's asking you to do than doing them. That was how I felt after a while, as one of the volunteers, as if I would be letting down the whole audience if I didn't play along. Besides, as soon as you don't perform, you are whisked off the stage by one of his assistants. He'll bring up a dozen volunteers because he knows he's going to lose some of them; some subjects simply reach a threshold beyond which they're not willing to go.

Let me help you understand what's going on in these situations by giving you clear definitions of "hypnosis," "self-hypnosis," and "hypnotherapy." Just keep in mind that my definitions are somewhat nontraditional and specific to the Essential Healing process. *Hypnosis* is a method of achieving an altered state of consciousness by guiding the mental mind to release its grip and step back, giving access to the subconscious mind and allowing consciousness to expand beyond the limits of the mental mind. *Self-hypnosis* is a self-induced therapeutic state of hypnosis that helps you achieve an expanded state of consciousness and become the objective observer, which I'll explain in a moment. Finally, *hypnotherapy* is the therapeutic application of hypnosis to deliver suggestions to help change behavior and to achieve expanded states of consciousness. As your consciousness expands beyond the limits of the mental mind, you become more of an objective observer with a higher perspective of yourself, the world, and the cosmos/universe. This allows you to more easily perceive and interact with various parts of yourself in a much more objective way. The process also helps you recover memories stored in your body and in the deeper layers of the mind that we generally call the unconscious or subconscious mind, the soul, or the superconscious. In highly expanded states of consciousness, free of the limits of the mental mind, you cannot only remember but also reexperience the unconditional love and oneness we all long for.

After a volunteer does something really embarrassing onstage, for example, the stage hypnotist usually gives them an out by saying that they have amnesia and won't remember anything they just did. The hypnotist stacks the deck by making something that would normally be undesirable seem desirable. That's a key to a successful hypnotic show because, during hypnosis, primarily two things occur: the mental mind steps back, giving access to the subconscious, and the person becomes more highly suggestible.

In hypnotherapy, as practiced by a trained, credentialed hypnotherapist, once you enter that state of relaxed mind, suggestions can be effective to change unwanted behavior, such as smoking or overeating—but only if the suggestions are desirable, believable, and achievable. This is why, for instance, some affirmations are more effective than others. For someone who is trying to improve their financial situation, repeating the affirmation "I am a millionaire" is usually not effective because it's not credible. But if instead they say, "Day by day, I'm becoming more prosperous," they have a much greater chance of success.

By the same principle, hypnotic suggestions will not work if they are aimed at getting you to do something that isn't desirable or that you do not believe you can achieve. Likewise, the hypnotherapist cannot make you do something against your will. To understand why that is, we first need to appreciate that the person in hypnosis is not asleep or unconscious; instead, they are in a state of expanded consciousness beyond the confines of mental mind. Let's face it, the mental or rational mind is limited and is bound by its limitations, which is why we need to gain access to a deeper level of consciousness. In hypnotherapy, people will accept suggestions to help them change behavior—especially toxic, self-destructive behaviors—but they will not accept suggestions to do things they would not normally do. If someone comes to see me and says, "My husband wants me to quit smoking," my first question is, "Do *you* want to quit smoking?" If they don't, then all the hypnotic suggestions I can muster will have no abiding effect.

Before lightning struck, my career as a certified medical hypnotherapist included a lot of therapeutic success. I started out working in a medical office treating clinical illnesses ranging from chronic pain and insomnia to fibromyalgia, and helping to modify self-destructive behaviors like smoking, overeating, and bulimia. Sometimes I would see eight to ten people a day, and I loved using hypnotherapy to heal their ailments but had begun to question the efficacy of treating symptoms that often returned after a short time. Then one day a woman came to me who had been suffering from shoulder pain for more than seven years.

Diagnosed with tendonitis and bursitis, Jeanie had tried physical therapy, chiropractic, and prescription painkillers without getting any lasting relief. When she was finally advised to have surgery, she decided to try hypnotherapy as a last-ditch attempt to avoid going under the knife.

As I was taking Jeanie into a deep trance to get to the root of her pain, she began describing an unexpected dreamlike scenario in which she had been a slave. Her master had been providing her and her son with so little food that her son was slowly starving to death. One night in desperation, she sneaked into the master's house and stole some bread to feed her son. The master caught her in the act and beat her to death. In the process, he stomped on her shoulder and crushed it. When I brought Jeanie out, she looked shocked, but said that her shoulder felt much better. Simply reliving the story, after seven years of being treated fruitlessly, seemed to make a big difference. I didn't know if what had happened was fantasy, psychosis, or a true memory of a past life for Jeanie, but when she reported months later that she was still painfree, and after similar healings occurred with several subsequent clients, I knew that I needed to learn more about regression.

The concept of using hypnosis to regress a patient back to early childhood and then to a previous life was fairly radical in the early '90s. But I studied the writings of Brian Weiss and Roger Woolger, both of whom had written classic books about past life regression, and in 1996 I took a course in the treatment from the National Association of Transpersonal Hypnotherapists. Although many people then considered past life regression too *woo-woo* for a medical professional, I had good success with it, and my clientele was growing. But I had also been learning to occasionally stop and enjoy the little pleasures in life, like driving my son to a summer swim meet in picturesque surroundings…only to be struck nearly dead. As I was recovering, scraping to pull myself back together into some semblance of a functioning human being, hypnotherapy proved to be a profound personal ally in addition to a professional one.

The Insights of Reliving a Near-Death Experience

Eight months after I was struck by lightning, I sponsored a workshop by a fellow hypnotherapist named David Quigley, who teaches a technique he calls Somatic Healing. Some years before, Quigley had learned how to heal himself from crippling rheumatoid arthritis and chronic allergies, among a host of other conditions. In the process he had trained as a hypnotherapist and, having restored his own health, had been teaching Somatic Healing in California using a combination of hypnosis and regression therapy. When he met me, David sensed that I was still suffering from the aftereffects of my lightning strike and offered to work with me as part of his demonstration. David believes that we store trauma in the body, and his techniques focus on locating and releasing it.

In front of a small group of sympathetic students, he suggested that he regress me to the moments just before the lightning struck to see if, together, we could locate the origin of my continuing pain. He asked me to lie on a gymnastic pad on the floor, and as I got comfortable, he began to gently regress me to the event.

The first image that came to me was one that had been recurrent since the lightning strike. I saw myself setting Orion down in the street next to the car, opening the door, and placing him on the front seat. With this image came the realization that had he stood in that spot a few seconds longer, he would have been killed by the lightning strike. That image began the process of reliving the entire event in very slow motion. David, supported by the whole group, skillfully guided me to the moment the lightning entered my body. By going through the event again, this time in slow motion, I was able to feel, over a period of about three hours, what had taken at most a fraction of a second.

As I regressed further, my feet began to tingle, and then they shook, slowly at first, then more and more violently. The shaking rose up my legs following the same course the lightning had traveled. Ten or fifteen minutes into the regression, my legs shook harder and faster than I could have possibly moved them if I had been trying. I may have looked like someone having a grand mal seizure. As the shaking rose into my hips and back, my whole body began to convulse, undulating on the floor in wave after wave of release. Each wave brought me more memories of the excruciating pain I had experienced. But each wave also released more of the trauma held so tightly in my muscles and nerves.

I remembered that as I was being electrocuted, the lightning pushed through my body in waves, each pulsation bringing me closer to what I was sure could be death. At this point David encouraged me to *welcome* the lightning into my body. I thought he was being crazy or perhaps a bit cruel. But he later explained that, as I had fought the lightning with all of my strength when I was hit, a lot of the energy and trauma was still stuck in my body. It became clear to me during this process that the back pain I had been experiencing since the strike was connected to the tremendous unprocessed energy that had become lodged in my back. Letting go and letting that tremendous force pass through me was exactly what I needed to do, like expelling a jagged piece of shrapnel from an old wound.

As I stopped fighting and "welcomed" the lightning into me, my body began to relax. The violent shaking and convulsing gradually subsided. And then came death. Supported physically and emotionally by the group, I curled up into a ball and went into a fetal position lying on my back. Everything grew dark, and I entered that great void, that "nothing" place that some people report in their near-death experiences. I remembered once again silently screaming "*No!*" I don't know how much choice I had in the matter, but as far as I was concerned, there was no way that I was ready to die yet.

From that quiet, peaceful void, I heard David quietly guiding me to ask why. Why did this happen? What was I to learn from it? And in that moment, I knew that it was because I was loved. Yet, even as that thought came to me, I questioned it. "Loved? *This* is how you love me? What kind of love is that?"

Just then I felt an overwhelming sense of gratitude from all those people whose lives I had touched in doing healing sessions and workshops over the years. It was almost as if a stadium full of my patients had stood up as one to cheer. All that gratitude filled me with such a feeling of worthiness, of being of use to the world, that I was profoundly uplifted—and, in a sense, relieved. My life was of more value than I had imagined.

The release gained by welcoming the lightning and pain continued to mushroom, slowly undoing the terrible damage that one hundred million volts of raw power had wreaked on me. As the feeling of relief and release mounted, I experienced being in what I have come to call the "Universal Sea of Consciousness," completely enveloped by unconditional love. During that experience, I felt connected with all life but, oddly, without losing my sense of self. Many of the accounts of mystics and others who have had experiences of divine or cosmic union often sound as if their personal identity was subsumed by the feeling of being One with everything, and it essentially disappeared. That wasn't what I felt, and simultaneously having a sense of self and no sense of separation from others was a life-changing experience.

That awareness makes it much harder to do harm. It makes you much less judgmental. Later, after I emerged from that regression, I recognized separation as a core wound that we all carry. This illusion of being separate often causes us to bury the sense of utter union that we experience in the womb.

In that overwhelming swell of unconditional love and oneness, a message came to me. "Listen," it said. Whether this was a recall of what I had experienced during the stretched-out time lapse after I landed on my head or the voice of guidance that came to me after I stopped fighting the lightning and welcomed it into me, I couldn't say. I didn't "hear" a voice in my head. It was more like a thought stream silently lighting up an idea that might have come from a spirit guide or from my own higher self. "Listen to spirit. You have a wonderful mind, but don't rely on it too much. Meditate, turn inward, and listen. Spirit speaks to you constantly; all you need to do is listen. Listen with your heart. Listen with your body."

Flooded with love for all that I was and all that I had done to help others, I began my return journey back into my body. Almost three hours had passed since the beginning of my regression, and I felt completely transformed, like a baby starting a new life. I came back into my body with the realization that, even when the body is unconscious or maybe clinically dead, a part of us is fully alive, observing everything. I had never had a problem with the concept of reincarnation because it made more sense to me than the conventional Western belief in heaven and hell. But actually surviving a kind of death made it real for me. That's where my search began. I knew in that moment that I would have to discover a way to help other people have that same kind of profound experience without needing to die, or nearly die, in order to have it.

Diving Through the Layers, into Your Soul Essence

Through the inner opening I experienced on the beach the day I turned forty, my lightning strike near-death experience, and my session with David Quigley, I have been able to dive into myself, burn all the way through those encrusted protections, and encounter a slowly mounting inner flame that continues to grow within me, which I have come to identify as my "soul essence." That soul essence at the core of our being is the image and metaphor that will ultimately guide you through the stages of your journey in this book.

The table below will give you a sense of where we'll be going through the course of the book. You might think of these nine layers more as a series of concentric circles, although it's easier to read them in this linear format. I should point out that the first five layers consist of a number of blockages, but also contain resources, such as the heart and the wonder child, whereas the last three layers are largely composed of spiritual resources that you will gain access to once you pass through the outer blockages. This table shows you the basic characteristics of each layer, and you will understand them more fully as you work your way through the book. Of course, you can return to this table at any time to recall the path. We'll cover one layer in each of the nine chapters that follow. Along the way, I'll be guiding you with a series of practices to help you move through each layer. By the time you're done, you will not only have an experience of your soul essence, but will also have learned valuable exercises that you can continue to use after finishing the book.

THE NINE LAYERS

Layer/Chapter	Elements of the Layer
1. Mental Mind	Thinking, analyzing, conscious interference, limiting consciousness
2. Heart	Feeling, giving and receiving love, doorway to inner world, protection
3. Stored Emotions	Retreating to safety of mental mind, getting triggered, driving behaviors, forming beliefs, survival strategies
4. Inner Child	Wonder child, wounded child
5. Parts	Old programs, archetypes, subpersonalities, things you have come to believe about yourself
6. Baggage	What you carry for others, inherit, give to others; soul loss
7. Inner Wisdom	Beyond intellect, the Body Wisdom Process, wise one within
8. Soul Memory	Knowing, superconsciousness, life purpose, lifetimes of learning
9. Soul Essence	Wisdom, unconditional love, oneness, inner guidance, guides

I developed workshops that were inspired by my en-lightning experience, which I honed over twenty-some years of working with thousands of people. While I've applied many of the same techniques I used in my hypnotherapy practice, I adapted them to go not just to the source of a physical ailment or toxic behavior, but to go all the way to the core of our being. This is the essential self that I discovered during that day on the beach when I turned forty and encountered again during my near-death experience, the part of us that I believe to be beyond time and space—to be, in a word, immortal.

To gain access to our soul essence, however fleetingly at first, requires making a deep dive through the nine layers outlined in the table above, some of which we have constructed over the years precisely to separate us from those nagging feelings of self-distrust or negativity that we work so hard to suppress. Throughout this book, I present practices for connecting to your soul essence, developing superconsciouness, and healing from trauma and other pain to live from the essence of you: a source of unconditional love and wisdom. Using the practices I present, you will travel from your mental mind, through the heart protection into your heart, where you will find stored emotions and your inner child. As you continue deeper within, you will discover and work with various parts of your psyche and the baggage that has kept you stuck, until you reach your inner wisdom, soul memories, and ultimately, your soul essence.

Superconsciousness is a level of awareness I will guide you into that perceives both material reality and the energy and consciousness that underlie that reality. The superconscious mind, which is synonymous with your soul, encompasses your essential self, and it is the source of your spiritual impulses, including compassion and the drive to achieve heightened awareness. The best way to use the extraordinary powers of the superconscious mind to live vibrantly in tune is through intuitive practices based on adaptations of self-hypnosis techniques and the use of expanded states of consciousness, which allow you to open channels of communication between your conscious mind and your superconscious. I have refined these practices over the course of decades and present them in the following nine chapters so you can perform them on your own.

This practical form of self-care also allows you to review your life and your development as a spiritual being—somewhat analogous to the so-called "life review" that people report during near-death experiences—as you find your path to healing and spiritual insight.

Along the way, I tell stories and share experiences from my clients and workshop attendees to illustrate how these teachings and practices have helped other real people like you. As I walk you through the program, you will move organically from one layer to the next until you connect with your soul essence and learn to stay in touch with it. In the end, you will own the journey in a personal way, and you will be able to use it to guide you through many kinds of challenges and troubling conditions in everyday life.

My experience with hypnosis and past life regression therapies has shown me how to help people move out of their head, dive through the layers of protection surrounding their heart, and ultimately go deep enough to get in touch with their soul essence. Through this book, you can discover the source of your pain—whether that lies in your body, in your mind, in your heart, in your personal and family history, or in your soul—and you can release and heal it so there are fewer and fewer layers blocking the expression of your soul essence. True healing means connecting with the soul essence and healing from the inside out. So, prepare to connect with your superconsciousness and heart, and to engage your intuition, as these are the pathways that will awaken the wise one within and lead you to your soul essence.

On your journey to soul essence, you will pass through each of the nine layers, clearing blocks or finding resources that assist you on your path. Some layers may require more work and repetition of the associated practices, while others may require less attention on your journey toward your soul essence. Once you reconnect with your soul essence and it begins to emerge from that place deep within you where it resides, it will help you heal from within, breaking through the emotional pain and trauma that have kept you stuck.

CHAPTER 1

Break Your Protective Trance by Moving Out of Your Mind

Many people walk through life in a type of mental trance. Working in New York City for many years, I saw how easy it is to go all day—buying lunch, getting a cup of coffee, taking the subway—without making eye contact, saying a word to the people I encountered, or even truly tasting my meals. The trance can seem like a solution to navigating a fast-paced, overstimulating environment day after day.

In my work as a medical hypnotherapist, I found that many of my patients were also in a kind of trance, and I had to find a way—unique to their condition or illness—of waking them from it. People who suffer from fibromyalgia, for instance, often become entranced in order to avoid their rising pain levels. The pain has become so much a part of their life that, as much as they want it to stop, they often come to feel helpless and walk around in a dazed fog.

Others suffer from various kinds of emotional pain that manifest physically. I worked with a number of bulimics, usually young women, who were suppressing powerful emotions. People who have bulimia are overwhelmed by negative thoughts and feelings. They feel guilty, or they feel ugly, or both. They also go through a lot of internal debate: Should I eat, or shouldn't I? Should I vomit, or shouldn't I? Almost always, however, the negative emotions dominate the internal dialogue to produce their version of a trance state.

The beginning of the essential healing journey is to break the trance you fall under to cope so you can begin to heal. We all pretty much strive to ignore our feelings or, if we can't manage that, to suppress them when they keep surfacing. It doesn't seem to matter if these feelings are guilt and shame or a nagging sense that we're not doing what we're supposed to be doing in life.

We call emotions "feelings" because they are accompanied by a corresponding physical sensation in the body. For instance, how do you feel grief? I experience grief as a sinking, contractive feeling in my chest. When our mind denies that such feelings exist, we can cause ourselves physical or psychological harm. Destructive habits, such as smoking, drinking, and compulsive sex, are often the result of avoiding feeling. Under the pressure of fighting these emotions, people often go into a kind of altered state—a trance—and act out irrationally by bingeing or self-harming. As long as we ignore the message from the body, the body will keep upping the ante, raising the volume until it gets our attention.

What may seem to be a simple accident or injury almost always has a deeper message behind it. If you repair the injury or toxic behavior without addressing the underlying source, it will eventually return. With bulimia patients, I learned to go against the grain and try to get them to feel the emotion that was causing their behavior. I asked *where* they felt the pain: in their belly, their chest, their throat. A patient would place her hand wherever she felt guilt or anger or fear, and then we tried to find a safe way for her to trace it back to its source. This is a process I call "presence-ing," in which we become aware of what we are actually feeling so we can work with the sources of our symptoms. For bulimia, I came up with a novel treatment plan: I taught patients to vomit. By that, I mean that I taught them to vomit their emotions instead of regurgitating their food. And once they did, they didn't need to throw up their food.

The journey from head to heart to soul in the course of this book begins by diving from the rational or mental mind, the first layer, that keeps us in a self-absorbed trance, down to the layers of safeguards and protective armor that we've constructed around our heart. When our heart feels threatened, many of us seek refuge in our head because we feel safer there, setting up a kind of negative feedback loop that keeps us stuck. This is why we can repeat the same inappropriate and ineffectual behavior over and over—we are so wrapped up in thoughts that we're disconnected from the inner wisdom that would guide us to take a better course of action.

To release yourself from the trance of your mental mind, you need to avoid the seductive urge to retreat to the security of the rational thinking that sidesteps emotional pain.

Expanded Consciousness: Reaching States Beyond Mental Mind

Mindfulness is all the rage these days, but I prefer *mindlessness!* "Out of your mind" is a good place to be. When I speak of the mind here, I mean the rational or mental mind, synonymous with the ego. (I distinguish it from Big or Cosmic Mind, which Larry Dossey and others often use as a term to refer to the universal consciousness that all humanity shares and which I tapped into during my near-death experience.) We overvalue intellect and education—which are necessary, but not at the cost of blocking out our emotions, and more importantly, our inner wisdom. As a result, we are stuck in our minds while our hearts stay closed, shut down, disconnected. The rational aspect of our being intends to help us perform successfully in the material world, but constantly critiquing ourselves paradoxically erodes self-esteem and worsens the very thing it seeks to protect.

In trying to deal with our endless thoughts, we often make the mistake of seeking to quiet the mental mind with various strategies, including meditation. More often than not, however, that doesn't work because most people haven't been trained to meditate or don't feel they have time to make it a daily habit. Instead, they end up making an enemy of the mind by trying to beat it into submission. Something similar happens when we try to forcibly silence the ego mind that hounds us, especially if we've suffered any kind of trauma early in life. I define trauma as an emotionally overwhelming experience or physical injury that leaves a wound—which is the meaning of the Greek root of "trauma." Like some physical wounds, traumas often leave a kind of scar tissue, and part of the scarring is that we feel alone and isolated with pain. This is obvious in cases of sexual abuse, in which the abused person is fearful of telling anyone, but it's true even of a car accident or disabling illness. The seeds of trauma can be planted in many ways: living with alcoholic, drug-addicted, or mentally or chronically ill parents, but also having your parents go through a divorce (which is true of half the population of America), having a chronically ill sibling, or something seemingly as minor as being berated by a teacher for missing an assignment.

I had a client who was an extreme speed bike racer, an apparently fearless guy with tattoos up and down both arms, who could zoom around a racetrack on his motorcycle with his knee almost dragging on the ground. And yet, he had such a fear of fireworks that he couldn't take his four-year-old son to a pyrotechnic show or even hold a sparkler. When he reached the origins of his fear, he recalled a fireworks display his parents took him to when he was nine, where he felt very afraid and wanted to leave. His father teased and then humiliated him by telling him to "be a man." At that point he became so agitated that he peed his pants and was punished by his father.

That seed, planted in the fertile ground of his subconscious, grew over time and was reinforced by several experiences with friends and his father—such an experience is called a "subsequent sensitizing event," or SSE. The SSEs intensified his phobia in a way that carried it into adulthood, but the initial cause had remained hidden in his subconscious until he gained access to it. This is how something that seems minor can become exacerbated in the subconscious over time.

The reemergence of a long-forgotten or seemingly minor traumatizing event demonstrates the dynamism of your neural network that connects your intellect and perceptions with your emotions. That event, no matter how far in the past, can trigger a phobic reaction. In order to heal the negative impact of embedded traumas, you can navigate the pathways involved. But first you need to learn how to go beyond your mind's protective instinct.

When I started doing the essential healing work of going "out of my mind," I found that my mind was concerned that something bad would happen if I totally let go of my thoughts. Over time, I realized that my mind *works* for me rather than *being* me, and as a result, I could feel my mental mind back off a bit. Your mind would love you to believe that all you are is *it*. But you are much more than your mental mind. The truth is that it's afraid of losing control because part of its job is making logical sense of things, and it can feel threatened at the thought of letting go of control. But that is exactly what you need to do to free yourself from the grip of emotional pain resulting from trauma. You will find it liberating to expand your consciousness beyond the restrictions of the mental mind's controlling nature.

You may have heard the term "expanded consciousness" associated with the use of synthetic drugs or psychotropic plants, such as psilocybin, ayahuasca, and cannabis, but you don't need any of those to expand your mind's ability to open into higher levels of consciousness.

Don't expect some mind-blowing high, however. You'll know you're moving in the right direction when you begin to feel the calm abiding presence that you may have experienced in meditation. If you have never meditated, it's simpler than many people make it out to be. Let your eyes go gently out of focus for a while, not thinking of anything but not distracted either. Then, closing your eyes, simply follow your breath as you breathe deeply and slowly. Imagine yourself sitting in a safe, comfortable place, perhaps a lovely meadow with your back against a tree, your mind absorbed in the sounds of birds while feeling the breeze.

PRACTICE: Out of Your Mind

Breathing deeply and slowly, relaxing your body, inviting your mental mind to step back and release its grip, your consciousness begins to expand. As your consciousness expands, you can begin to relax enough to observe what your mental mind is saying. As you become the observer of your mental mind, you become more free of the mental mind's limitations, opening a doorway to your subconscious mind and its much vaster dimensions. This expansion of consciousness is the foundation of virtually all the practices we will do in this book.

This technique of expanding your consciousness is part of both hypnotherapy and meditation—which are different vehicles, and included in the practices that follow—that share the goal of allowing you to slow down from the rapid pace of everyday life and gain access to your subconscious and, ultimately, the superconscious mind.

One helpful effect of expanding your consciousness is that you can begin to use your mental mind as it is intended—to help you function in daily life. Your mental mind also helps you to implement, in a practical way, the insights and direction you receive during more expanded states of consciousness that result from following the practices we'll be doing in this book. You need to know that even the sharpest intellectual mind has limitations; for one thing, it can't comprehend certain aspects of consciousness or even of material reality. This is especially true in the case of trauma. People get stuck trying to figure out trauma because sometimes there is no *why*. Traumatic events and their aftermath don't make rational sense, so we often get stuck on the *why*. "Why did my mother do that to me?" You're trying to make sense of nonsense, but you can't. You are trying to make logical sense out of what was an illogical action or behavior.

If we make an enemy of the mental mind, it digs its heels in even deeper, so we need to relax it before we can find ways of working around it. Your rational mind is likely fearful that it may recall something traumatic in a way that will retraumatize you instead of healing you, so it blocks your access to the heart and emotions. I call this "conscious interference." Neutralizing it entails a few basic steps.

Relax Conscious Interference

When you become aware that your mental mind is interfering, ask it if it has a specific concern and what its concern is. Concerns may be simple things like discomfort or a distracting noise outside, in which case you can adjust your environment, rearrange your seating, or close the window. But some concerns may have to do with more serious worries, like the one I just mentioned—that something bad may happen if your mind "loses control." If you feel your mind becoming locked down in fear, you should first acknowledge and thank your mental mind for its important role in keeping you alive all these years. Then gently say that this introspective work is necessary for you to do, and ask it to go sit in a chair and simply observe and record what's happening.

You can't make your mental mind disappear by suppressing it, but by not attacking it and instead offering something to occupy it, you can start to see beyond its protective trance. The conscious, mental mind can do only one thing at a time, so if you give it something to do, it will leave you alone. That's one reason why we traditionally use bells, candles, and mantras in spiritual practice to distract the conscious mind and let us gain access to the deeper levels of our subconscious, or what some call the higher self.

This can initiate a cascade of healing responses: when you consciously take a step back and become the observer of your mind, your mental mind grows quiet, often for the first time in your life, giving you a chance to make contact with your subconscious mind. The subconscious is a multitasker—it stores memory and emotions and runs the autonomic nervous system, which acts largely unconsciously to regulate bodily functions, such as heart rate, digestion, respiratory rate, and sexual arousal. So whenever you find that your mind is resisting, throwing up barriers, making negative statements, or otherwise numbing you so you can't access your emotions, give this conscious interference the task of becoming an observer and recorder. Essentially, take it off center stage so you can open to other levels of consciousness.

Evoke Your Relaxation Response

The term "relaxation response" was created by American cardiologist Herbert Benson, who was approached in 1968 by practitioners of Transcendental Meditation, a version of traditional Indian meditation promulgated by Maharishi Mahesh Yogi. The practitioners insisted that they could control their blood pressure by entering a meditative state. Benson agreed to study the practitioners as long as he was free to publish all of his findings, pro or con. As it turned out, Benson discovered that the participants were indeed able to lower their blood pressure by meditating. At the time, most physicians still believed that the cardiovascular system was completely autonomic and could not be consciously controlled, so this was a significant breakthrough. Benson also ascertained that simple relaxation techniques derived from meditation could reduce respiration, heart rate, and brain activity and that meditators did not require any spiritual beliefs (although he didn't discourage them either). Benson ultimately adapted the practice of meditation to a secularized format that he called "the relaxation response" and, in 1975, published his findings in a popular book of the same name. We'll see why this ability is significant shortly.

Generating feelings of safety and calm offers a foundation that will allow you to engage the practices you'll learn in this book. One key to counteracting the fearful, overprotective mind is to create a "safe place" for the mind to go, based on memory or imagery, which can be visual, auditory, kinesthetic or feeling, gustatory, and olfactory. We will use all of them, although the first three are the most common. This encourages your body to release chemicals and brain signals that make your muscles and organs slow down and increase blood flow to the brain. And, if you run into a past trauma on your inner journey and find it overwhelming, you can retreat to safety in an instant. If you are prone to anxiety and even panic attacks, this will also help reduce the number and severity of attacks by easing your fight-or-flight response so you remain relaxed.

To even begin to learn how to get out of your mind and into your heart and superconsciousness, you must first be able to induce your own relaxation response. In this section, I'll share several ways to do this so you can explore and see which works best for you. Or if relaxing is a true challenge, you can combine them all into one process with stages that will take you progressively deeper into feelings of safety and calm.

Establishing a Safe Place in Your Mind

Imagining yourself in a place where you feel safe elicits the same relaxation response often generated by meditation or visualization. What is your safe place like? It may be a favorite beach or hiking trail, a temple or stained-glass chapel. Maria, a gifted concert pianist, had such serious stage fright that she sometimes made glaring mistakes when she performed with a prominent state symphony orchestra. The condition became so serious that she would sometimes read a book while performing to distract herself. Her safe place evoked several senses at once. Maria chose a peaceful meadow in which she could feel the warmth of the sunlight on her face, smell the grass and flowers, and watch butterflies flitting around her.

PRACTICE: Finding Your Safe Place

Close your eyes and take a couple of deep letting-go breaths. Recall a time and place where you once felt calm and safe. It can be a real place, like a place in nature, a home, a temple, a chapel, or other sacred location, or an imaginary place, like the holodeck of the *Starship Enterprise*. (It shouldn't be in the arms of a parent, a lover, or any other person who might evoke a situation of dependency.) Using all your senses as vividly as possible, imagine being there. Maybe you feel the warmth of the sun, melting tension from your body; maybe you smell the flowers or cut grass; there may be the sound of gentle waves or soothing music. Luxuriate in the special "ahhh" feeling you get from being there.

Once you have soaked in the safe surroundings and familiarized yourself with this environment, it will be helpful to create an "anchor" so you can recall your safe place in an instant. An anchor can take many forms: a drawing or image, a key word, a physical action, or a combination of these.

Maria needed to evoke the comfort of that safe place while she was busy playing in rapid-fire synchrony with an entire orchestra. Clearly Maria couldn't touch her fingers together when they were flying across the keys, so we developed a "toe press" that she could first invoke before she went on stage. Then, as she pressed the pedals with her toe while playing, that reactivated the anchor, and she felt the soothing environment of the meadow wash over her. She rarely, if ever, made those conspicuous errors again.

PRACTICE: Creating an Anchor for Your Safe Place

In creating an anchor for your safe place, begin by using your senses as vividly as possible to imagine yourself in the safe place you chose in the previous practice. Once you feel that you're there, while pressing your thumb and forefinger together, say silently to yourself several times, "I am safe, right here, right now." Holding on to the good feeling of being in your safe place, allow your thumb and finger to come apart. Then allow your eyes to open, feeling safe, calm, and relaxed.

As with any new skill, in order to reinforce the anchor, you should practice it a few times when you're in a nonstressful situation, say, in your bedroom or meditation room. Then you can use it in any situation where you feel anxious, whether it's on a crowded bus or train, on a plane, or even at a party or meeting where you feel uncomfortable.

The effect of having a safe-place anchor is often virtually immediate, definitely faster than antianxiety medication, and can also help you face situations that you find unpleasant. Growing up, I had a brutally inept dentist who rarely gave me enough Novocain, often drilled my gums, and generally inculcated in me a fierce dread of dentistry. As a result, as an adult, I put off going to the dentist as long as I could, and when I did go, I would need twice the normal amount of Novocain *as well as* nitrous oxide—no matter how skillful or gentle the dentist might actually be. My anxiety, of course, made it even harder for the dentist to do his job. After I learned hypnosis, I developed my own safe-place imagery to use before and during visits to the dentist.

The very first time I tried this, the dentist noticed the difference and wanted to know what happened. "I used half the Novocain I normally use, and I didn't turn on the gas at all," he said in astonishment. "And you were so much more relaxed than when I used double Novocain *and* gas." After seeing how effective the safe-place imagery was for me, he referred many of his patients to me, and I was happy to help them, too, get beyond old painful experiences.

Feel Safe in Your Body

Some people find simply suggesting that they visualize a safe place doesn't always work. When you attempted to find a safe place, you may have felt too exposed at the beach, for instance, or were fearful of getting lost in a forest, or even felt claustrophobic in a meditation hall.

People who suffer from chronic pain, anxiety, and related conditions, such as fibromyalgia or post-traumatic stress disorder (PTSD), often find that merely visualizing a safe place doesn't always work. They have often been on high alert for so long that they can't easily reset their alarm system. When you live in a state of constant perceived danger, you may develop a kind of radar to detect any possible threat. A child who grows up with an alcoholic or drug-addicted parent often develops a number of strategies to stay safe. They may become hyperaware of danger signals, like the sound of stumbling feet, angry voices, or the smell of alcohol on the breath. Over an extended time, their system remains on high alert, and they become hypervigilant.

Hypervigilance can also cause physiological responses that are painful. Even if your fear is illogical, you will still feel the same painful symptoms as if you were facing an armed intruder. For instance, a large percentage of people with hypervigilance suffer from insomnia. When you're constantly on red alert, your body releases powerful chemicals that keep you super alert—and then make it difficult to relax into a sound sleep. When those chemicals, such as the hormone cortisol, are released over an extended time, they can have a damaging effect. As your body attempts to protect itself through a continuous, needless triggering of the fight-or-flight response, it generates any number of symptoms and actually puts you more at risk of physical damage.

When our mental mind is so consumed by a constant state of alert, it's a little like what happens when you don't have enough RAM on your computer—it freezes up. Continuously scanning for danger can also prevent you from responding to a safe-place practice. I developed the following practice to help you reach the threshold where you can finally start to relax. If you have struggled with various physical illnesses, anxiety, or panic attacks, see if this practice helps empower you to cope with those states on your own—and to begin to access the state of super-consciousness that will help your spiritual journey unfold.

PRACTICE: Reminding Your Body "I Am Safe"

This practice helps bring your mental mind back to a more neutral place in the present moment. Working with individual parts of the body is often far more effective than giving yourself generalized instructions, such as "Relax!" Mental mind tends to dwell on the past (regrets) or the future (fear of the unknown), so it never feels safe.

Begin by allowing your eyes to close and taking a few relaxing breaths. Breathe deeply, drawing the air down into the abdominal area so you can feel your belly expanding as you inhale.

Continue the process of relaxing both mind and body, turning inward, and allowing your consciousness to expand beyond the limits of mental mind. Letting go of past misgivings and future worries, focus on the present and send a message of safety to three important areas of your body.

First, send a message to your feet and legs, speaking very softly or even silently to yourself, slowly and deliberately, pausing briefly between each word or phrase: "Feet and legs...I am safe...right here...right now." Repeating this phrase a few times, let your feet and legs relax as completely as possible.

Next, tell your hands and arms: "Hands and arms...I am safe...right here...right now. Hands and arms, you can relax...and release...and let go." Now let your hands and arms relax as completely as possible.

Next, say to your spine and nervous system, "Spine and nervous system...I am safe...right here...right now. Spine and nervous system... you can relax...and release...and let go." Now let your spine and nervous system relax as completely as possible.

Savor the feeling of unwinding, unclenching, and softening at your core. Repeat the "I am safe" message as many times as you need to; then feel how your body responds. If it tenses or rebels, repeat the message, going more and more deeply into relaxation.

Each of us has certain places in our body where we tend to store tension and worry the most. If you feel tension or anxiety emanating from another part of your body—your jaw, stomach, shoulders, or forehead—you can repeat the same process for those areas.

Intentionally set aside time to do this practice on an ongoing basis. As you become more familiar with the feeling of safety in these key areas of your body, you will create a bodily memory. This is a good way of retraining your mind and body both to be at a lower level of alert and to feel safer. Eventually you may find that the words "I am safe" can trigger an instantaneous relaxation response. You can take this a step further by learning to use the "control room" of your mind to reset your overall level of alert.

PRACTICE: Resetting the Protective Alert Level of Your "Control Room"

We all have an internal warning system, and it is usually set to one of three levels: green for calm and relaxed, yellow for caution, or red for immediate danger. When your system is set on green, the body can renew and rejuvenate itself. You feel more focused and more comfortable in your own skin and are able to sleep better and digest better. Yellow, or caution, is for rare occasions when you perceive an immediate threat of serious injury. And red alert is reserved for very rare occasions when you perceive an immediate threat of being killed or dying.

Clearly, green—calm and relaxed—is ideal most of the time. However, you may have set the warning system to a high level out of necessity, probably sometime long in the past. The flight-or-fight response is such that it happens automatically, bypassing the thinking part of the brain. You may have maintained that setting even after the actual threat had gone, perhaps for so long that you are not even aware of it.

Once you determine where your system is set, you can recalibrate it as needed using "the control room" of your mind. This practice will guide you through that process, which will be followed by safe-place imagery.

Begin by imagining that your consciousness is just the right size to travel anywhere inside your body (something like the 1960s science fiction film *Fantastic Voyage*). You may imagine yourself as a tiny vessel or simply an abstract awareness, like a colored light or smoke.

As you travel through your body, move into the control room of your mind. There is an area with a large panel that has knobs and dials and gauges on it. In the center of that panel, locate a very special section labeled "Emergency Warning System." Check in and see where your system is set.

If it's set on yellow caution or red alert, take hold of the Emergency Warning System control and turn it down to a level more appropriate for right here, right now: green for calm and relaxed.

Now that you have turned down the control setting, send the same messages that you sent to your arms, legs, and spine ("I...am...safe... right here...right now. You can relax...and release...and let go.") from the control room down through your entire body like gentle waves of relaxation.

Now, using all of your senses, as vividly as possible, imagine yourself being in a place where you feel safe, calm, and relaxed. It may be a beach, forest, garden, or other natural environment, or it may be a spiritual setting where you feel safe, such as a church, temple, mosque, shrine room, or home altar. Imagine a spot there where you can sit down and enter an altered state of consciousness, allowing your consciousness to expand beyond the limits of your mental mind. In this place, you can rest and simply be.

As you finish this practice, feel into your body and become aware of your physical presence. Open your eyes slowly and take in your immediate environment. Take a few more relaxing breaths and prepare to go about your business of the day.

You can always return to your safe place when you feel your system moving into the yellow or red alert level. "I...am...safe...right here...right now." These are powerful words because when they reach into your physical body, they have immediate physiological effects that you can observe through awareness. This is similar to the feeling of having one aspect of your awareness observe other aspects in meditation. You may have even felt this outside of a meditative experience, as it's a common occurrence and isn't especially mysterious. What's happening is that the observing aspect of the mind is working at a higher or expanded level of consciousness, and the observed aspect is the mental mind, or more simply the ego. You can learn to develop this process of self-observation, even without learning how to meditate.

Witness Your Mind as an Observer

Your goal of achieving an expanded state of consciousness is to further your essential healing. Your goal is not necessarily to quiet destructive behaviors—although that may happen—but to expand consciousness beyond the confines of the mental mind. In this state, consciousness enlarges, and you become the objective observer—you achieve a state sometimes called "witness consciousness." You may have heard the term "witness consciousness" before; self-help author Wayne Dyer wrote about it extensively, and the phrase itself can be traced back to the ninth-century Indian spiritual master Shankara. Which is simply to say that, although "objective observer" is a method used by many of today's hypnotherapists, it is actually based on ancient wisdom and on tried-and-true contemporary practices.

The practices in this chapter can be brought together to form the basis for your essential healing process. They are how you can achieve a higher perspective beyond that of the everyday ego or mental mind. These practices may overlap and interconnect during any given practice session, and their intensity may vary over time. For now, let's bring them together so you can experience how to get "out of your mind" and into your essential healing state.

PRACTICE: Feeling Released from Thought

The primary requirement for this practice is to be in a place that is relatively quiet and where you can be free from intrusions. Then you'll begin by exploring what it's like to be in a relaxed and open state of awareness.

Allow your eyes to close and take a few deep relaxing breaths. Breathe deeply, drawing the air down into the abdominal area so you can feel your belly expanding as you inhale. Begin the process of relaxing both mind and body, turning inward and allowing your consciousness to expand beyond the limits of mental mind. Relax your feet and legs; next, relax your hands and arms; relax your neck and shoulders; relax your face, your jaw, your mouth, your eyes, and your forehead.

Now, using all of your senses, as vividly as possible imagine that you are in a place where you feel safe, calm, and relaxed. It may be a beach, forest, garden, or other natural environment, or it may be a spiritual setting where you feel safe, such as a church, temple, mosque, shrine room, or home altar. Imagine a spot there where you can sit down and enter an altered state consciousness, allowing your consciousness to expand beyond the limits of your mental mind.

Now take a few moments to observe your thoughts. Just notice what you hear your mind saying. Allow your thoughts to come and allow them to go. Notice the freedom of feeling released from your thoughts. Enjoy the expanded state of consciousness that you've achieved for a few minutes.

As you finish this practice, feel into your body and become aware of your physical presence. Open your eyes slowly and take in your immediate environment. Take a few more relaxing breaths and prepare to go about your business of the day.

I find it best to do this practice in the morning or evening, but you should choose a time when you don't feel pressured. You may want to do it regularly as you work your way through this book, integrating it into the other practices.

When you observe your mind, generally one of three things will happen. Your mind may be quiet, it may voice a concern, or it may try to assist you by suggesting that you relax. Here are some ways to respond:

- If your mind is quiet, that's fine; enjoy the silence!

- If it tries to interfere with you—for instance, by suggesting that this whole process is a waste of time (what I described earlier as conscious interference)—then thank it and let it know that while it serves you well in your day-to-day life, what you are doing here is beyond its ability, and it can best assist you by stepping back and letting go. So, ask it to sit down next to you and just observe and record.

- If it voices a concern, however, you will need to address that. Begin by asking your mind what it's concerned about. You don't need to do this out loud, but listen to what your mental mind has to say. The two most common concerns are to keep you safe or to question your ability to do this correctly; in the latter case, you can tell your mental mind that it's not designed to do this kind of work. Your mind may also complain about noise or discomfort, in which case you should adjust your environment accordingly.

- If it's feeling unsafe, you can create a "safe place" where you can go at any time during these practices or whenever you start feeling anxious or threatened, like you did in the "Finding Your Safe Place" practice. When you repeat this practice later, you may find that your safe place changes from time to time depending on your mood, and this is perfectly fine.

Releasing from thoughts and becoming an objective observer is a living, ongoing practice that will evolve, and you may find less resistance as you become more comfortable with it. Conscious interference may occur any number of times while you are doing the practices throughout this book. The key is to learn how to get your mental mind to leave you alone long enough to expand consciousness and get on with the stages of your awakening.

Essentially, if your mind says that it doesn't want to delve into your pain, ask it to step back enough to let you proceed. Ask it if it has any concerns, and if so, address them. You can adjust any minor distractions, but if your mind becomes overly fearful, just acknowledge and thank it for helping you survive. Then gently say that this work is necessary and ask it to assist you by sitting in a chair and simply observing and recording what's happening.

When you can observe your mind, free from conscious interference, you become the objective observer. You are ready to step out of your mind and continue to expand consciousness. You'll find that repetition will make it ever easier to let go of your mental mind. This will serve as the basis, or jumping-off point, for all future practices in the book as you continue to move closer to the soul essence at your core. Indeed, you can use this process of releasing from thought at any time to prevent your mental mind from distorting or blocking other exercises. Note that some of those exercises may take you very deep into a relaxed state, so it's important to leave a little time at the end to transition back into your more accustomed active state of mind.

This chapter has been devoted to preparing you to achieve expanded consciousness in a way that you can repeat whenever you need to. Any time you become aware that your mental mind is interfering, you now have tools to counteract it.

CHAPTER 2

Enter Your Heart, the Doorway to Your Inner World

Do you find anything so painful, whether emotionally, psychologically, or physically, that you are in denial about it? When we encounter painful feelings and repressed emotions, we may retreat to the analytical mind and try to "think" our way through them. As you learned in chapter 1, this is counterproductive because it results in a kind of mental trance that prevents us from living fully. This strategy of ignoring the pain escalates as we withdraw from it and finally seek to anesthetize it. To counter that impulse, you want to enter into relationship with the pain: to explore it, feel it, dialogue with it, and to express it in a way that won't cause harm to yourself or someone else.

Lawrence was a financial adviser in his forties who had been very successful in his career but felt empty in much of the rest of his life. He was particularly dismayed that his romantic relationships never seemed to go well. After speaking with him, I realized the problem. Lawrence was so stuck in his mind that he couldn't find a single emotion that he could identify. He needed to get out of his analytical mind and into his heart. But when the heart is closed and so profoundly shielded as his was, that can be hard to do. So, I had Lawrence follow the process I described in the last chapter: close his eyes, take a few breaths, and tell his mental mind to go sit down and just take notes. As he relaxed during the breathing, he revealed that, a few years before, he'd experienced an emotionally devastating breakup with a woman he had hoped to marry. And since then he had difficulty feeling anything.

I asked Lawrence to place a hand on his chest, over his heart. He said that he could feel the weight and warmth of his hand on his chest. The next thing he felt was tightness. Having a physical sensation is often the prelude to feeling an emotion—and as he focused his attention on that tightness, he began to feel a deep sadness. Slowly at first, Lawrence sobbed; then he cried uncontrollably over the loss of his fiancée. As he cried, his heart opened, and then we were able to begin the journey inward.

By doing the opening practices I'll share in this chapter, Lawrence grew more comfortable feeling his heart. As a result, he was not only able to understand what had been behind the failure of so many prior relationships, he also embarked on a journey toward understanding his deeper nature—his soul essence.

Once we move out of our rational thinking minds and into our hearts, we can process the hurts and wounds we carry and begin to feel love again. The goal in this chapter is to open your heart, the next layer in the process of Essential Healing and the doorway to the inner world, as you move from thinking to feeling. Here, I don't mean the physical organ of the heart, but the center of feeling that is located in the middle of the chest. The challenge is that, when you move out of the mind to the heart, you will likely run into the heart's protection, a kind of armoring we often develop early in life that shields the heart from pain.

PRACTICE: Feeling into Your Heart

We spend so much time in our head that we don't often enough spend time identifying with our heart on a regular basis. By placing your hand over your chest, you are better able to move your awareness from your thinking mind to your feeling heart.

Allow your eyes to close and take a few relaxing breaths. Breathe deeply, drawing the air down into the abdominal area so you can feel your belly expanding as you inhale. Bring your attention to the center of your chest, the center of emotion. Place your hand over your heart center. Invite your heart to open, feel into your heart, and notice what you're feeling. Ask yourself, "What am I feeling right now?"

This is a simple practice to repeat throughout the day as a way of becoming more familiar with your feelings at any given moment. We usually know what we're thinking, but not as often what we are feeling.

Explore Your Heart Protection

The challenge is that, when you move out of the mind to the heart, you will likely run into the heart's protection, a kind of armoring we often develop early in life that shields the heart from pain. We all have some form of heart protection; some of us, like Lawrence, may be so deeply protected that we are no longer even aware of what we are feeling. When I'm training therapists for regression therapy, I tell them that no matter what techniques they may have learned for inducing hypnosis or deepening that state, if their client's heart is closed and shielded, then they're not going to get very far because the heart truly is the doorway to the inner world.

It's essential to work with this heart protection, which all of us have, and to identify the particular form that it takes. It most likely had a function that once served you, but now it may have outworn its purpose and is causing pain and isolation. Having a substantial level of protection not only holds in the old hurts, locking them down, as it were, but also makes it harder for us to connect with others on an emotional plane. That might even mean not being open to love when it presents itself.

If you're currently in a situation that still requires substantial protection, for instance, a relationship—with a partner, parent, child, or coworker—in which you feel threatened, abused, or at risk in some way, you may need to maintain the heart protection you have in order to stay safe. That's okay, as it is important to protect yourself. You can still invite your heart to soften enough to give you access to it, with the understanding that you don't need to open it to anyone else at this time. This will still allow you to go in and reconnect with the feelings and inner wisdom that reside in your heart.

Get to Know the Protection

The accumulation of heart protection over the years may make it difficult to open your heart or identify feelings, so it can help to objectify your heart protection to allow you to make a deeper connection with your heart. "Objectification" simply means to see or sense something, even an emotion, as an object of some sort. Some people will identify depression, for instance, as a heavy, dark, cold blanket or see rage as an explosive ball of fire. Once you can name something, you can interact with it—get your hands on it, so to speak. The following practice will encourage you to ask, If your heart protection were an object with a particular size and shape, color or texture, what would it be? Some people describe their heart protection as a steel door, a brick wall, or barbed wire. Others say it has a rotting or putrid odor or makes a loud crackling or buzzing sound, like an electric force field.

One client encountered steel doors guarded by laser guns, constantly scanning the perimeter to zap potential invaders. I suggested that, rather than immediately trying to disassemble the laser guns and steel doors, she first thank them for keeping her safe. After all, they had kept her feeling secure for quite a few years, and although the need for them had passed some time ago, they were still operating. When she thanked them, as often happens, the protections softened and became more permeable. This way, she was gradually able to gain access to her inner world.

Because the coping strategies that generated your protections may no longer be necessary, I suggest that you notice what condition the object seems to be in. Some people find their protective shield is old and rickety, while others may characterize it as well-preserved.

PRACTICE: Identifying the Objects That Protect You

Developing a relationship with the protection is essential because it will help you identify the source of the protection and explore what made it necessary. As you did with the mental mind in the previous layer, which also served a certain protective function, you will begin by thanking the protection for keeping you safe for so many years. Once you acknowledge and thank the protection, you can then pass around or through it.

If your mind feels overactive at any point during this practice, apply what you learned in chapter 1 and ask it to take a seat aside from you to simply observe and take notes. And if for any reason you feel unsafe, you can use the "Reminding Your Body 'I Am Safe'" practice. I will suggest that, at a certain point, you place your hand over your heart for a time. Then, if at some point you feel more comfortable relaxing your hand at your side or in your lap, of course that's fine.

It's likely that in doing this practice for the first time, you may experience feelings bubbling up. When the heart has been closed for a long time, you may feel a sense of relief as it begins to open up again. Following this initial relief, long-held sadness often may arise, usually followed by a deep sense of love. If these emotions do arise, just relax and let them flow. They provide the raw material with which we will work in the next chapter, where you will work with the emotional layer.

I recommend that you acquire a journal or notebook to record your responses to the practices in this book. You don't need a fancy journal; a spiral notebook or composition tablet will do, as will a digital file if you prefer.

Allow your eyes to close and take a few deep relaxing breaths. Breathe deeply, drawing the air down into the abdominal area so you can feel your belly expanding as you inhale. Begin the process of relaxing both mind and body, turning inward, and allowing your consciousness to expand beyond the limits of mental mind. As you continue breathing, relax your feet and legs; next, relax your hands and arms; relax your neck and shoulders; relax your face, your jaw, your mouth, your eyes, and your forehead.

Take a moment to observe your thoughts. Notice what you hear your mind saying. Next, bring your attention to the heart center in the middle of your chest, the center of your feelings and emotions. Breathe into this heart center and invite it to open. You might place your hand on your chest to make the connection palpable. Allow yourself to become aware of whatever protection you may have around your heart.

Take another deep, letting-go breath and ask yourself, "If the heart protection were an object, what would it be?" Notice what size and shape your protection takes. Notice as well its condition. Does it seem sturdy and secure or a bit worn and rickety? How does it feel to have it there?

Then ask the protection these questions and listen to what it says. Write the answers on a sheet of paper or digital device:

- What is your purpose?

- How do you protect me?

- Who do you work for?

- When did you come into my life?

- What made you necessary?

After noting your protective object's responses, thank it for having kept you safe for so long. Upon thanking it, it will generally soften and relax.

By continuing to function as it has, the protection actually causes you pain. While holding in old hurts from the past, it's also preventing new love from coming into your life. Although you don't want to get rid of it, you do want to transform it into a more malleable, permeable form of protection. When we open our hearts, we become vulnerable. To function in the everyday world—taking the subway, making business transactions, even interacting with certain family members—we need some protection. What's more useful is a dynamic form of protection that can change with the circumstances.

The aperture on a camera lens can be a helpful metaphor. An aperture opens and closes depending on the amount of light in the atmosphere so as not to allow the image to be distorted. In the same way, you can open or close your heart to varying degrees as needed. Without losing the ability to open our heart to those we love or want to help, we can still use discernment to adjust the opening and avoid being harmed. We don't have just a binary choice, wide open or wide shut, but rather a range of options.

When protection has been in place for a long time and we modify it by making it more flexible, we may need to check in with our heart during the course of the day to see how the new protection is working out.

Learning to Listen to Your Heart

When I was undergoing my near-death experience, I received the strong message that I have a good mind but that I tend to rely on it too much. I got the point that I need to listen to my heart more—and doing so has transformed my life. We spend all day listening to the voice of our mind telling us what it thinks. And yet, how often do we listen to what our heart is feeling? I'm not saying that we should stop heeding the mind; it serves a valuable purpose. However, I feel we need to reorder our priorities.

We are actually better off reversing the usual order: listen first to what your heart wants; then consult the mind to figure out how to make that happen. If your heart says it wants to spend more time in nature, ask your mind how you can do that. Maybe it will suggest that you take more weekend trips out of the city, or maybe it will tell you to become a forest ranger. Your mind is good at finding solutions to problems, but your heart is much better at letting you know which problems you really need to solve.

PRACTICE: Clarifying Your Heart's Voice

In your journal, draw a circle, and divide it into four quadrants. The two on the left are "My mind thinks"; the two on the right are "My heart feels." The top quadrants are "now," and the bottom quadrants are "future." Think for a moment about some of the things you need right now, and write those in the upper-left quadrant. Then, in the bottom-left quadrant, write down a thing or two you think you will need in the future.

Now, place your hand on your chest, breathe and feel into your heart center, and feel what your heart longs for most right now. Write or draw that in the top-right quadrant. Then, feel what your heart most desires for the future, and write or draw that in the lower-right quadrant. This way, the things that you think you need are listed on the left half of the circle, and what your heart longs for will be on the right half. For instance, your mind may be saying you need to work more toward making money, but the heart may be saying you need more time in nature.

Observe what you have written and drawn, and evaluate the difference between what your mind thinks is most important both now and in the future, as listed on the left half of the circle, and what your heart longs for, as listed on the right half. If you put your heart's needs last or ignore them, you will create an unbalanced life. If you pay attention to what your heart longs for and use your mind to accomplish it as best you can, then you will most likely be living a more fulfilling life.

When We Refuse to Listen to Our Heart

Beth had come to see me complaining of irritable bowel syndrome and a stabbing stomach pain that became worse during her period. She was married to a physician whom she met in med school, but she had given up her practice as a neurologist after they married and started having children—two boys, ages ten and twelve. They had been together fifteen years, but over the ten years since their second child was born, the marriage had devolved into more of a perfunctory relationship. Although her husband wasn't overtly abusive, as time passed, she found him seriously lacking in emotional warmth and connection. They rarely had sex, and Beth referred to her husband as "my boys' father." Perhaps because she had been in a previous relationship with a man who was physically and emotionally abusive, she found her current husband a relief. She was tempted to stay in the marriage simply because her husband was a good provider who gave her the freedom to do whatever she wanted and provided round-the-clock care for their younger son, who is autistic. "My husband isn't a bad guy," she told me. "I just don't feel anything anymore."

Beth suspected that her pain might be tied in some way to her dilemma, and after some work to get in touch with her heart, she resolved to leave her husband, and her stomach condition improved for some time. But she was ultimately unable to make the break, and over time her stomach illness returned worse than ever. It's often only a matter of time before the misery caused by ignoring our heart's urging becomes strong enough to make us listen.

The disparity between what your mind and heart say can lead to much of the stress you feel in your day-to-day life. What if you were to slow down for a minute at various times throughout the day, place your hand over your heart, and ask what it wants, what it needs?

PRACTICE: Encountering Your Heart

The mind judges emotions, but the heart can hold many emotions at once, including opposing ones—like love and hate. This can cause confusion when we try to identify the nature of a particular feeling. We need to keep in mind that emotions have corresponding physical sensations, and we may feel those sensations before we feel the actual emotions. Some people feel tightness in the chest, for example, as Lawrence did, or perhaps a knot in their stomach. When these sensations arise as you do this practice, just notice the feelings, breathe into them, and let them come and go. Don't judge the feelings, just let them be. Even though they carry pain, you can find a way back to love in your heart once you dissolve or bypass your heart protection. In time, learning to listen to your heart will open the doorway to listening to your soul essence.

Begin by going through the process of getting out of your thoughts. Visualize the object that you identified as your heart protection. Thank your protection for serving you well in the past.

Find your way around, over, under, or through the protective object. As you let down the protective shields and walls, at least for now, allow your heart to open to you, and begin your journey inward, deeper and deeper within this heart.

Once you are past the protection, notice how your heart looks and feels. Ask your heart what it truly needs and longs for, what it wants most in this moment. Ask your heart what it wants to show you or tell you.

Now replace the heart protection you originally found there with a more dynamic form of protection, one that is more permeable and that can change with the circumstances.

With your heart more open and maintaining your connection with the heart, gently and gradually return to your natural waking state.

PRACTICE: Viewing Your Heart Anew

The work you have done in this chapter is powerful, so I encourage you to write down what you have discovered in your journal, using the following prompts. Having this overview supports you in an ongoing way so you can make daily choices—big and small—based on what your heart needs and the messages it shares with you.

- My heart protection looks like: _____
- Having my heart protection there feels like: _____
- My heart protection exists to: _____
- It serves me by: _____
- When I go into my heart, it looks and feels: _____
- My heart needs: _____
- My heart shows/tells me: _____
- My new heart protection is: _____
- My heart wants to show me or tell me: _____

Piercing or melting the protection brings us face-to-face with our authentic feelings, and many people find this daunting. But feelings are just feelings—we need to let them come and let them go because holding on and internalizing them will cause emotional or physical illness. In extreme cases, they may explode outward in a damaging emotional torrent that often hurts the ones we love most. You may find that you need to open your heart gradually during this process. This is why the next chapter will help you learn to process and integrate your emotions.

CHAPTER 3

Unearth Emotions, Beliefs, and Survival Strategies

When I was four years old, I became very ill with an extremely high fever and swelling in my throat. At first our pediatrician thought I had the mumps, but it was not that. As my fever continued to climb, I was hospitalized and filled with antibiotics, but the fever persisted until I was delirious and near death. I have only vague memories of that very long week or ten days. Unbeknownst to me, my condition was so serious that the doctors informed my parents they should be prepared for the possibility that I would not survive.

That horrible fever finally broke, as mysteriously as it had come, but I was left completely paralyzed from rheumatoid arthritis. I spent the following year in Stanford Children's Hospital (then called the Stanford Home for Convalescent Children), being treated and rehabilitated. I was completely disabled. I could not pick up a pencil or hold a fork. I had to be wheeled around in a wheelchair. I couldn't even feed or wash myself. Although I received excellent care and my parents often came to visit, I was scared and lonely.

In the bed next to me, in the group ward that had become my home, was a very ill boy, whom I could barely see through the foggy plastic walls of the oxygen tent that surrounded him. Upon waking one morning, I saw that the oxygen tent was gone—and so was Jimmy. Jimmy didn't make it. His condition had worsened, and he had died during the night.

I wondered: *What happened? Where did Jimmy go?* And in my child mind, I worried, *Am I next?* At that point, I was really scared and felt even more alone. Of course, at that age, I didn't understand much about death. But I began to think, *What can I do to keep them from taking me away in the middle of the night? Maybe if I am really good and very strong, they won't come for me.* So I decided that I would survive by becoming good and strong. I call this kind of thinking "child magic."

After endless hot and cold baths, physical therapy, other rehabilitation, and lots of steroids, I was gradually able to walk again and hold things with my fingers. Later, my parents would often tell the story of the day in the hospital when I was finally able to hold a fork again and feed myself. After almost a year of these treatments, the arthritis that had crippled my body abated, and I was able to go home. That is a day I will always remember. I had a new sister, and we had a new home! My "child magic" had worked. I survived. They hadn't come for me in the middle of the night. In my child mind, being good and strong had paid off! Little did I know at the time that being good and strong would become my lifelong survival strategy.

And yet, four-year-olds shouldn't have to be strong and good. My strategy of being "good and strong" meant not being any trouble to my mother, who was on overload, as well as feeling responsible for my younger brother and sister. Above everything, I was convinced that I had to deny my feelings because if I did not, I would die. And if that becomes your survival strategy, as it did for me, it can lead to emotional conflicts later in life. Carrying that belief into adulthood, I didn't even know why I believed that I shouldn't ever feel tired and that I should always instinctively know what to do in any situation. And, in any challenging scenario, I should pretend to be strong and not ever show any weakness. Indeed, we need to do the opposite; we need to find ways to feel and express those emotions, the next layer in our journey to essential healing.

The Effects of Emotional Suppression

As we continue our journey to discover and connect with soul essence, we will examine primarily three things: our stored emotions, the limiting beliefs that grow out of those emotions, and the survival strategies that have evolved to cope with those beliefs.

One of the abundant benefits of modifying our heart protection, as you learned to do in the last chapter, is gaining more open access to our heart and to the many emotions that are stored there. All emotions demand expression. By their very nature, emotions want to be expressed. Feelings want to be externalized. Imagine feeling intense love for someone to whom you are close, whether a partner or spouse, parent or child, brother or sister. What would be the point of keeping your love holed up inside instead of expressing your feelings by embracing your loved one at every opportunity?

When we internalize our emotions, or in other words, when we do not express them, we miss an opportunity for a richer, warmer experience of life. And we also create stress. The same holds true for afflictive emotions, like anger and resentment. Suppressing these feelings often leads to illness.

Take sadness, for instance. When we feel sad, we often make matters worse by continually suppressing our feelings of sadness, and then they may eventually develop into depression. This is a significant distinction. We all feel sad on occasion; our sadness might result from learning about the death of a longtime friend or close relative, a setback in our work, or even a last-minute cancellation of a dinner with friends. That kind of sadness passes with time or in some cases may spur us to take action. But when we persistently feel sad based on suppressed anger or feelings of low self-worth, that accumulated sadness can create a reservoir of depression. People who relentlessly repress their feelings of sadness may eventually become overly fearful of experiencing any sadness at all and will try to avoid situations that can trigger that emotion or find ways to numb themselves. The most common vehicles for numbing ourselves are excessive drinking, overeating, and drug use, but there are also other, less obvious ways of numbing ourselves, such as shopping and gambling.

By uncovering the nature and constituents of your heart's protection, as you did in the last chapter, you can now move on to the next layer and engage the exposed and stored emotions, ingrained beliefs, and survival strategies that led to the construction of that protection.

Ways We Relive the Same Pains

With our heart open, we dive deeper, working with emotions and the resulting beliefs and survival strategies, which make up the third layer on our way to the core self. For instance, it's sadly common to feel that we have been unwanted, unloved, or abandoned. These feelings become entrenched as the belief that we're just not good enough or that there's not enough to go around. And then those beliefs become activated every time we're in a relationship because we want to avoid getting hurt again. So, subconsciously we adopt the survival strategy of leaving before they leave. Unfortunately, we then wind up feeling even more sad and alone.

Cheryl was having great difficulty in her marriage although she believed that her husband was "a good man." Asked to characterize her feeling toward men in the past, she expressed the belief that "they all leave." When she was quite young, her father left on a business trip, had a stroke, and died from an aneurysm, and she never saw him again. Her mother didn't take her to the funeral, so all Cheryl knew was that her father, whom she loved dearly, left and never returned. Her survival strategy was not to let anyone get too close because they would certainly leave and hurt her. This dynamic had now begun to play out in her marriage. Her husband constantly asked her, "Why won't you let me in?" To which she would respond, "Because you'll leave and hurt me again." He answered that her strategy was creating an emotional dynamic that might indeed give him a reason to leave, despite his love for her. Without releasing her stored abandonment emotions and her survival strategy of not letting anyone in, Cheryl will continue to perpetuate her loneliness. (We'll see in the next chapter a variety of ways to work with childhood traumas and devise more effective strategies for healing them.)

The subconscious will always win out over the conscious mind, so we need to explore and resolve our unhelpful patterns. Here again we will use the tool of objectification. Once the emotions begin to surface, we deal with them in a loving way. In this chapter's exercises, you'll learn how to see, feel, or sense these emotions as they arise. Feeling encompasses kinesthetic responses, and sensing is primarily intuitive. The goal is to encourage you to trust your inner knowing, which can take many forms that we'll soon explore.

Although our survival strategies grow directly out of our repressed emotions and the faulty beliefs we have generated to protect us from those emotions, these strategies don't really protect us from getting hurt. That is because they are essentially ineffective in either releasing the emotions or resolving the cause of the hurt. As we saw with Cheryl, if you have come to believe that all relationships inevitably lead to pain, you may develop the strategy of avoiding new relationships—or, if you do start one, of being the first to leave! Just as we are often unaware of our stored emotions and beliefs, we are also largely ignorant of how they lead to ineffective survival strategies because they operate primarily on a subconscious level. Once we have released some of our stored emotions, then we can begin to work on our beliefs and survival strategies. This allows us to choose more effective beliefs and strategies.

From Sadness to Depression

At one of my workshops, Julia said that she was afraid that if she started feeling her sadness too intensely, she would ultimately fall into what had become her vast reservoir of depression and never be able to pull herself out again. But the practices we engaged in during the workshop, which included several techniques for expressing and releasing trapped emotions and are discussed in this chapter, had a remarkable effect on Julia. Releasing her sadness allowed her to discover more of the inherent happiness within her.

There are many different kinds and levels of depression. It may start as inexplicable sadness—unexplained only because we are not consciously aware of its actual cause—but if not addressed, it can grow to a serious, even clinical, depression. Paradoxically, suppressed feelings also act as magnets that attract people or situations into our lives that will trigger those very emotions. When certain people perceive us as having low self-esteem, which may also be an issue for them (like attracts like), they may take advantage of a chance to dominate someone who appears to have an even lower opinion of themselves than they do.

The Emotions That Feed Your Self-Defeat

Our mental mind judges our emotions, which is one reason we bury them. We think, *I shouldn't be having these feelings*, or *I should be feeling another way*. As a result, they accumulate in the subconscious and the body. As noted earlier, we call emotions "feelings" because every emotion has a corresponding physical sensation. Remember, emotions are forms of energy that demand expression—we need to externalize them—but when we experience an uncomfortable emotion, we're more likely to internalize or suppress it.

This will generally lead to one of two things. It may contribute to or directly cause disease. Or, if enough suppressed emotions accumulate over time, they can generate an internal volatility, such that when we finally release the emotions, they may explode out of proportion to the particular event that triggers the release. Often, we direct these explosions at the people we love most. What we need is a way to express these emotions safely, that is, without harming ourselves or other people. The first step to doing that is to intentionally acknowledge what we're feeling.

PRACTICE: Finding the Seat of Emotions

The stepping-stone from blocking emotions to acknowledging them is to identify the physical sensations and locate where they live in your body. All it takes is three simple questions.

Close your eyes, take a few deep letting-go breaths, and ask yourself:

- What emotion am I feeling right now? (For example, anxiety.)

- Where in my body am I feeling this emotion? (For example, in my chest and belly.)

- How does this emotion look and feel there? (For example, tight and pulsing.)

Write down your answers to the three questions above. You can repeat this practice at various times when you sense an emotion coming up. You may find it helpful to date each entry. It's a great way to become more aware of when and why particular feelings arise in you and where they are located in your body. Linking emotions to sensations and to specific areas of your body will help you gain a more concrete sense of how they operate within you. This will also prepare you for the practices later in this chapter to help you release your emotions safely because, before we can release feelings, we first need to identify and locate them.

While doing the "Finding the Seat of Emotions" exercise, Barry felt his depression as a dark, heavy, wet blanket weighing him down all over his body. He sensed that the purpose of the blanket was to hold down his rage. As a gay man growing up in the South, Barry was tormented by bullies and felt humiliated by his sexual identity. The anger he felt toward his many tormentors was so overwhelming that he didn't dare express it for fear of making matters worse. When he finally left the South, he carried his rage with him and kept it suppressed. After he was able to release his anger using one of the techniques described below, he no longer needed the blanket of depression and was eventually able to let it go. We often try so hard not to feel our anger that we have no idea that it lives in the body or where in the body it registers. Everyone experiences anger in somewhat different ways and places: flushing in the face, constriction in the throat, turbulence in the belly. People often describe it as a kind of pressure or heat. Others describe a choking feeling, as if someone is strangling them. But the choking is actually cutting off the anger before it can be expressed. We are strangling our own emotion. You may even experience anger in different places at different times.

The following is a simple exercise you can do right now to identify how anger feels in your body and where you feel it.

PRACTICE: How Does Your Anger Feel?

Take a few deep breaths and close your eyes. Recall a time when something made you feel especially angry. Breathe and feel into it. Notice where in your body you feel the anger and how it feels there. What do you notice about it? Take another breath and then open your eyes.

Anger most often is held in the gut and chest, and when it's triggered and seeks an outlet, it usually moves upward through the body. As it rises up and you begin to feel angry, your mind may say, *"I shouldn't be feeling this. Anger is a bad feeling, or my anger is dangerous, and I shouldn't express it."* But then what do we do? Often, we stuff our anger, swallow it, internalize it in some way, which is exactly the opposite of what we need to do. What we mainly need to do with afflictive emotions, once we have identified them, is to express and release them.

Venting Your Pressure Cooker of Stored Emotions

Suppressing emotions can lead to diseases or disorders, and the way to avoid that is to find a safe way to release them. Think of the valve on a pressure cooker that allows you to release the pent-up steam safely; without the valve, the whole pot would explode.

The following series of three practices are safe ways to release your emotions. You may find one or more of them helpful, depending on which emotions are currently playing a role in your life. You may also discover that all three of these techniques can help you at different times and in different situations, so I recommend that you try each of them.

I also encourage you to devise techniques of your own that you may find even more effective. We can release our emotions in many ways—through writing, drawing, visualizing, and verbalizing or making sounds. Once when I was upset about something, my therapist handed me a tennis racket and encouraged me to beat a couch with it. To me, that felt contrived and pointless, especially with him standing there watching. Later, on my own, I found it far more effective to place my hand on my belly, where I felt my anger, and to imagine blasting the anger out of my belly like lava out of a volcano.

Once you bring your attention to stuck emotions, they will generally begin to move. Depending on the emotion, it may want to flow up or down to find its way out of your body. Heavier emotions, such as sadness, depression, and grief, may want to flow down and out. You can drain these feelings from your body like draining the water from a reservoir. But more volatile feelings, like anger, fear, and anxiety, may want to rise up and vent out of your body. As anger rises, you can release it upward, maybe blasting like lava from an exploding volcano, as I discovered. You can also vent it straight out like hot air from an exhaust.

PRACTICE: The Volcano Release

Using the volcano release is especially apt for anger and rage, which can be damaging if repressed. Ask yourself, "What's the driving force behind my anger?" Is it righteous anger, as at an unjust situation? Or is it irrational rage generated by an injured ego? Sometimes anger can be empowering, but if it becomes so highly charged that it prevents you from taking appropriate action, you need to defuse the anger so you can move forward. We can direct righteous or justifiable anger at a person or institution that we feel has treated us unfairly, or we may direct it at the injustice in the world. That anger can be constructively channeled into political or community activism, but the emotion behind the anger still needs to be safely vented. Some people get frozen and can't react to anger at all. But the key is to let it out in a safe way.

Close your eyes, place your hand on your chest, take a couple of breaths, and recall a situation in your life that is making you feel angry. With your hand in place on your belly, breathe and feel into the anger stored there. Notice how it looks and feels there. Breathe into it.

Now, imagine that you could gather up all the anger in your body and blast it right out of your belly or your upper body like lava blasting from a volcano. Release it! Let it blast, flow, ooze, pour, shoot, or run right out of your body. You may find that making some sound or even saying some words out loud will help you release the stored anger. As you blast it out, you can send it down into the earth or up into the sun, where it can be transformed or vaporized. You don't need it anymore. Let it all go.

PRACTICE: The Balloon Release

The balloon release may be most appropriate for a variety of feelings that seem to be trapped in different areas of your body. It can be especially helpful if you are having a hard time determining exactly what the emotions are or in which parts of your body they may reside. (If you like, after completing this practice, you may write down the names of the emotions that come up for you.)

Close your eyes, place your hand on your chest, take a couple of breaths, and imagine a situation in your life that is troubling you. Imagine that all the stuck feelings that you are ready to let go of around this situation are helium balloons. Each balloon is filled with one of the feelings that is troubling you.

Let the first balloon rise to the surface and float up and out of your body. As it comes out, notice that something is written on it. A kind of label or sticker on the balloon will say what feeling is in the balloon. What does that first one say?

With all those feelings filling that balloon, when you are ready, let it go. Release that balloon and watch it drift away. Push it away if necessary, and watch it drift farther and farther away. Higher and higher up—up into the sun where it is disintegrated, vaporized, gone forever. Let it go. Take a nice, deep, relaxing breath.

Now let the next balloon come up. What does that one say? Let all of those feelings fill that balloon. Now let that one go, too. Release it and watch it rise up farther and farther away until it, too, is vaporized. Repeat this as many times as necessary until they are all gone.

Now it's time to breathe into the space that you've created. Feel it fill with something more healing and nurturing like calm, love, or sunlight. You can use the word, the image, or just the feeling to fill that space.

Breathe it in, let it fill you, and rest in the comfort of that sensation. Feel your feet resting on the floor, grounding you, and allow your eyes to open gently. Take a few more breaths and prepare to go about the rest of your day.

PRACTICE: Releasing Your Burdens

The next practice is especially helpful and liberating if you tend to take on more than your share of responsibility. While you may not be able to shed the responsibility of taking care of an aging parent or a special-needs child, for example, at least you can relieve some of the emotional weight of the burden you carry. This is especially true if your role as caregiver is having a negative impact on your mental or physical health.

Allow your eyes to close and take a few deep, relaxing breaths. Imagine yourself walking along a beautiful mountain path. Notice the color of the leaves, the blue sky, and the sweet smell of the forest. As the trail turns up an incline, notice that you are wearing a backpack—a backpack full of all your burdens. They are all the burdens that weigh you down, that hold you back from being who you truly are, in the form of rocks. Feel the weight of those rocks. Notice how these burdens slow you down and make moving difficult.

When you are ready, stop there on the trail and open the backpack. Look in and notice all the rocks in the pack. Take the first one out and notice that the burden is written on the rock. What does that first rock say?

Now take that rock and get rid of it. Roll it off the edge of the cliff. Throw it away. Do it however you want to, but get rid of it. Let that burden go.

When it is gone, take out the next one and do the same. After you've thrown that rock off the cliff, take out the next, and the next, until they are all gone.

If you have trouble releasing one of the rocks, you can first explore the experience around the feelings. Set the rock down and work with it. Notice its size, texture, and color. See what it's composed of. Even have a silent conversation with it. After resolving the situation connected with the feelings in the rock, you will be able to throw it over the cliff or roll it away.

That's good. Now that all of the rocks are gone, you can take the backpack off and throw it away too. No need to carry any of those old burdens anymore. Feeling lighter and freer, you make your way to the top of the hill where you sit and meditate or just soak up the beauty and freedom of the view.

If you have had difficulty releasing your emotions through these practices, it may be that they originated before birth and, so, are harder to release. In this case, you may find the practice "Reparenting Your In-Utero Self" in chapter 8 helpful.

How Beliefs Grow Out of Suppressed Emotions

When we carry stored emotions long enough, especially from childhood, they often lead us to form beliefs of which we are not consciously aware. Besides our being unaware of the source of these beliefs, they are almost always untrue. We form them not through a rational process of self-examination and discernment—which can be beneficial if carried out consciously and without judgment—but in unconscious response to the accumulated emotions themselves. In part because we are unaware of their existence, let alone how they were formed, these beliefs exert an extraordinary amount of control over how we behave. Like the operating system of a computer, which is running a whole range of programs in the background while we are aware of only what we see on the screen, our unconscious beliefs control how we behave in the world. Some people call them "limiting beliefs" because they often constrain us in ways of which, again, we are unaware; as a result, we are unable to change them, even though they are usually wrong.

One of the most common beliefs we carry is some form of "not enough." That can take the shape of *I'm not smart enough, I'm not rich enough, I'm not attractive enough,* and so on. Another variation is *There is not enough—not enough love, not enough prosperity, not enough food—to go around.*

On a personal level, this belief expresses itself as, *I have to do something in order to be loved.* That can lead to self-limiting actions, such as saying yes to someone when you should say no. It can also lead us to want to please other people to win their love.

When we say or think, "There's something wrong with me," what we really mean is, "I'm not whole." This implies that we are incapable of changing our behaviors because we lack sufficient internal resources to control our actions.

In the next practice, you are going to look at some of the beliefs that have led you to develop certain behaviors and survival strategies. They are probably the same beliefs that are limiting you or causing you trouble.

PRACTICE: Finding Your Belief Statement

Here is a list of some of the most commonly held beliefs that may help you to identify some of your own.

- I am not enough
  - not good enough
  - not smart enough
  - not pretty enough
  - not manly enough
  - by myself.
- There is not enough
  - not enough money
  - not enough food
  - not enough for me
  - not enough time
  - not enough love
  - to go around.
- I'm unlovable.
  - No one can love me.
  - I don't deserve love.

- I am not needed.

- I am not wanted.

- Something is wrong with me.

  - I am defective.

  - I am broken.

  - I am weird.

  - I am damaged.

  - I'm too sensitive.

  - I don't belong.

- I don't deserve / I'm not worthy of

  - love

  - care

  - attention

  - respect

  - to be seen

  - to be heard.

- I'm not safe / It's not safe.

  - The world is not safe.

  - People are not safe.

  - It's not safe to succeed.

  - It's not safe to trust.

  - It's not safe to be happy.

Although you may relate to several, pick one or two that most closely fit your basic limiting belief about yourself. In your journal, write down your belief statement. For instance, if you chose *I am not smart enough*, and *There is not enough money*, write, "I believe I'm not smart enough, and there's not enough money."

Consider what activities result from this belief. Record these in your journal by completing the following: *Because I believe I'm not smart enough and there's not enough money, what I tend to do is…*

What is the survival strategy that drives these actions? For example, "I tend to pick jobs for which I'm overqualified and underpaid, so I'm always in debt. I don't believe I can afford to get training or a higher degree so I can get a better-paying job." Write about your strategy in your journal.

The Sources of Your Underlying Beliefs

Most of our misleading beliefs are based on childhood events that may be traumatic, but some simply stem from ordinary life experiences. Unfortunately, we often remain not only unaware of the beliefs but also ignorant of their source. You may be aware of your misguided beliefs, but you need to go further and identify and root out their original cause. Some people like to track these beliefs to their religious upbringing, but that's not necessarily the primary influence. Familial beliefs play a role, and in many cases, our parents and grandparents developed their own beliefs based on how their parents treated them and then passed them on to us. This is a subject we'll discuss in depth in chapter 6.

The first time I gave a public talk about hypnosis was at a rotary club in Tuxedo, New York. I was so nervous after I arrived that I couldn't go on at first. So, I went back outside and sat in my car and did some self-hypnosis. The image that came to me was an event that occurred when I was about eight years old. One day when my father came home from work, he got angry that I left my bicycle in the driveway and he couldn't park his car there. My father was an airplane mechanic, and he usually wore overalls, but that day he happened to be wearing a suit. He was also usually pretty gentle, but for whatever reason, maybe extra stress at work, he was short-tempered that day, so I had incorporated the image of a man in a suit towering over me and criticizing me in no uncertain terms.

Sitting in my car in Tuxedo before my talk, I realized that eight-year-old Paul was trying to figure out how to give a talk to a group of men in suits and get it right, filled with the same anxiety that he had felt that day with his dad in the driveway. I told my eight-year-old self, "Adult me knows much more about hypnosis than you. I can do this. You go play in the forest in your safe place." When I went back into the hall, I was a different person. I was the adult-professional me, not the scared kid—and I gave a great talk.

In the next chapter, we'll explore your relationship with the younger you, often called your inner child. For now, it's enough to understand just how vulnerable that child felt at the time and how our fearful beliefs often arise from our fear of losing the love of others, beginning with our parents.

PRACTICE: Tracking the Past Experience You Are Still Living

Select one of the belief statements you created in the practice above. Let's say you chose *I have to be responsible.* Ask yourself, "Why do I have to be responsible? What am I afraid will happen if I am not responsible?" Your response may be, "Everything will fall apart." Then feel into your cause-and-effect belief statement, for example: "If I'm not responsible, everything will fall apart."

> Close your eyes, take a few deep breaths, and ask yourself, "How does that feel?" Follow that emotion of fear back to one of the first times you can remember feeling it. Take a few more deep breaths and repeat to yourself, "If I'm not responsible, everything will fall apart" (or whatever your response was). Now, vividly remember yourself in the situation that generated your fear of everything falling apart.

Record in your journal the experience that led to the need to be responsible and your fear of everything falling apart.

It's likely that many of the past experiences you're still living through your beliefs involve your parents or primary caregivers. In a child's eyes, parents and caregivers loom as godlike figures. In a classic example, the parent comes home from an exhausting day at work and yells at their child for spilling a glass of milk, which, in that moment, can lead the child to feel devastated. The child may form the belief that they're not good enough, not worthy of their parent's love. If this kind of scene is repeated often enough, it's more likely to create suppressed emotions and a resulting false belief. But that process can also result from a single event, as happened to me. The child develops a survival strategy of doing whatever it takes to get back in the parent's good graces.

Beliefs Turn into Survival Strategies

Ask yourself what survival strategy you may have developed to get back in your parents' good graces. It may have been in response to a seemingly minor "offense," but it nonetheless has carried an undue weight in your life. For instance, if you wrote, "If I'm not responsible, everything will fall apart," then your survival strategy would likely be to be overly responsible.

Sara came to see me with her husband because he never took responsibility for paying bills or keeping the house in order, even though he made good money as a news cameraman. When she did this practice, Sara recalled that her parents were party animals who often invited their friends over to drink and get high. But they never cleaned up after themselves, and Sara was confronted by the mess they left. Her strategy was to take on the responsibility of cleaning up after them. She had even lived through having the power turned off because her parents had ignored the bills. Although Sara couldn't sign the checks herself, she learned to open the bills that came and make sure her parents paid them.

As an adult, Sara attracted partners who were party boys whom she had to clean up after—a perfect match for her need to be overly responsible. At some point, of course, she would get pissed off at her partners for always having to clean up their messes! Her current husband fit this mold perfectly. When he forgot to pay the electric bill and they received a late notice, she became furious and insisted that they go for counseling. Her husband also realized that her anger wasn't so much about his being wrong but about an ineffective survival strategy that his wife had developed. He agreed to carry more of the weight around the house and take more responsibility for paying the bills.

PRACTICE: Tracking How You Decided to Survive

To track the steps by which your beliefs were converted into survival strategies, apply this template to your insights. In your journal, substitute your own strategies and beliefs for the examples in parentheses here.

- If I'm not _____ (strategy: responsible), I am afraid that _____ (belief: everything will fall apart).

- If I'm _____ (strategy and belief: not responsible and everything falls apart), I am afraid that _____ (deeper belief: the power will be shut off).

- If I'm _____ (not responsible, everything falls apart, and the power is shut off), I'm afraid that _____ (deepest belief: we won't survive).

- Ask yourself, "What does that remind me of?"

- This reminds me of _____ (origins of belief: my parents being irresponsible and our power being turned off).

- In that moment, what I decided I needed to do to survive was ___ (how you decided to survive: always take responsibility).

Now that you have tracked how your belief led to a specific survival strategy, let's look at how that strategy has been influencing your life since then. You probably have a primary strategy that will jump out at you, and you should address that one first. But if others arise, you will find it helpful to track those as well.

The Hidden Motivation Beneath Survival Strategies

Our survival strategies generally begin to form early in childhood, when our reliance on our parents is close to absolute. If they withhold their love or condition it on certain behaviors, we are likely to adjust our conduct to meet their demands. Part of seeing them as godlike figures stems from our literally depending on them for our survival, which leaves us with very limited options. We can't move out because where would we live? We can't force an unloving parent to be more loving or an alcoholic or addicted parent to stop drinking or using drugs. And although we are working with restricted resources, we still need to find ways to get our parents to love us and to keep us safe. If we had the perspective of an adult, we might simply grit our teeth and say, "There's nothing more I can do," but as children, we often come to mistakenly believe, *It's my fault, and I should be able to do something about it.*

Children aren't aware of the fact that nobody should have to behave a certain way in order to get love. And so, we once asked ourselves, *What can I do to get my parents to love me?* We responded, perhaps unconsciously, with, *I'll be good, I'll be funny,* or *I'll please them however I can.* Sometimes these strategies work, and sometimes they don't, but they are all we have. Yet, even when they worked, they left you at a disadvantage. Your clown strategy might have helped you win your father's love, but then you would be assuming an artificial persona to gain something that should be your due as a child.

We all need to give and receive love, but that giving and receiving can come from a place of freedom, not out of a desperate need to survive. A further problem is that once we develop these survival strategies, we carry them into our adult life. We continue to be the clown or pleaser trying to win or earn love from everyone in our life, we keep playing the bully or victim to stay safe, or we remain the peacemaker so everyone appears happy. To heal this cycle, we start by acknowledging that we can't go on being a people-pleaser or a clown to earn love from anyone, not just from our parents, or being the bully, victim, or peacemaker to protect ourselves from dangerous people or situations.

In some extreme cases of having to cope with parental dysfunction, because we couldn't leave home on an external level, we may have left internally, by dissociating in a variety of ways. Similarly, these kinds of strategies become our internal operating system, running in the background of our life without our being aware of them. It would be much more helpful to respond to each new situation as it arises, using creative problem solving, instead of robotically replaying an old strategy from our childhood that is no longer effective.

What we really need is to develop more effective strategies that draw on our inherent strengths and capabilities. In place of survival strategies that are fear-based and chosen from a very limited range of possibilities, we would be better off developing strategies that arise from who we truly are at our core—our soul essence.

How Beliefs Lead to Guilt

One of the most common variations on the theme of *I'm not enough* is *I'm guilty. It's my fault.* This belief implies that something is inherently wrong with us, and feeling guilty can invite others to blame us. A young woman named Aparna took time away from her successful medical practice to oversee the care of her father, who was being treated for kidney cancer. She felt an intense love for her father, which he returned. However, she had always sensed that her mother didn't share her dad's love for her.

After seven years of struggling with cancer, her father died, and although he had lived much longer than most patients with his kind of cancer, she was left feeling, *I didn't do anything for him. I didn't try enough treatments. There was an experimental treatment plan I should have gotten him into but couldn't.* Aparna felt so much responsibility for her father's health that she neglected her own family and let her own practice suffer. She had carried this sense of responsibility from childhood because her mother made it clear that she had wanted a son, not a daughter. Her strategy to win her mother's love and acceptance was to do more and be better than anyone else. She was first in her class, went to medical school, and became a successful physician—because that is what her mother would have wanted their "son" to become.

When we are helpless to change who we are to make someone happy and it's impossible to make them happy, we can attract blame from that person. This even spreads to a spouse or other family members, as if we carry the target of guilt on our back. The thing is, if you wear a target by feeling guilty, the blamers are encouraged to fire volleys of arrows. Once they've gone into attack mode, nothing will stop most of them. It's true that you can't eliminate the archers, but you can shrink the target by releasing your guilt. Then they can blame you all they want, but their arrows won't be able to find the target.

When Aparna did the practice to release her guilt, described below, she came to realize that the reason for her exaggerated sense of responsibility was *I am only a girl*—her variation on *I am not enough.* But through the practice, she understood that it was not her fault that her father died and that she had done everything in her power. On an even deeper level, she realized that she carried so much guilt for not having been born a male that she had spent her life overcompensating. By discovering that she believed that she was lacking because she wasn't a boy, Aparna was able to identify the source of her survival strategy—trying to win her mother's approval by doing more than anyone else. She recognized that she was a deserving person, even without her mother's approval, and that *It's all right to be a woman!*

Realizations come not so much from discussing your situation, but by releasing the guilt you feel. Doing so begins by identifying where in your body you feel the guilt.

PRACTICE: Shrink the Target of Guilt

To let go of guilt, first become aware of the guilt you carry. Identify where in the body you feel it. For instance, I feel guilty in my gut—it's a corrosive and contractive sensation in the area of my solar plexus, the site of self-esteem. Guilt is one of the most common targets, but you can adapt this exercise to your own target, such as victimhood, weakness, *not enough,* or *always wrong.*

> Allow your eyes to close and take a few deep breaths. Recall a time when you were feeling especially guilty, whether as a child, an adolescent, or adult. Breathe into it. Notice where in your body you feel guilt and how it feels as you recall it.

Record the sensations in your journal.

Whereas anger is fiery and tends to rise, guilt is often heavy, so when you release it, you can let it flow down into the earth. As you begin releasing the long-held guilt, another layer of belief may arise around why you *shouldn't* release it—because something bad will happen if you do. If this comes up, just continue to release as much as possible. Then, you may find it helpful to go back to the "Finding Your Belief Statement" practice to work with this new layer of belief you have touched upon.

> Now breathe into the area where you feel guilt. As you inhale, visualize the air going to this place in your body, expanding the sense of space around it. You may find it helpful to place your hand there. Let the corrosive, contractive guilt feeling begin to ooze out. Just let it drain out for as long as necessary. Notice how it feels to let the guilt go. Then, when you feel complete, let your eyes open.

You can use this practice anytime someone tries to make you feel guilty for not being who they want you to be. It can take as little as thirty seconds. You don't need to hold onto guilt or other afflictive emotions, and releasing them requires that you feel them as they move on out of your body. The point here is not that you shouldn't feel things or that you need to get rid of negative feelings, but that oppressive feelings don't have to accumulate and linger as they did in the past.

Now, if something makes you feel angry or guilty in the moment, you are equipped with ways to release the anger or guilt and let go of it. You can even do this with your eyes open, on the spot, in any situation.

Archetypes of Survival

High school and middle school are good places to observe survival strategies in action because by then, we've already begun to solidify them. In the pressured environment of adolescence and puberty, we are perhaps more than ever aware of and vulnerable to what our peers think of us.

If you consider your time in middle and high school, you can probably identify some of the most common archetypes of survival that you and your peers took on. For instance, you may recall the pleaser, who would seemingly do anything to fit in and make the kids like them. The class clown is related to the pleaser because, while they may be genuinely entertaining, their humor serves to ask others to like them, while concealing their own insecurity. Another variation on the pleaser is the rescuer, who may make it their job to "save" other people as a way of winning their undying gratitude. Paradoxically, the rescuer is often the person most in need of rescuing.

PRACTICE: Identifying Your Survival Style

Here are a few of the more common personas or archetypes that can be applied to the survival strategies that we adopt from childhood and carry into adolescence and adulthood. Although you may find several, pick one or two that most closely fit your basic survival strategies and write them in your journal. If yours is not included here, feel free to find one word that describes it.

- Bully
- Pleaser
- Martyr
- Hero
- Peacemaker
- Manipulator
- Hypervigilant one
- Cheerleader
- Entertainer
- Victim
- Responsible one
- Caretaker
- Overachiever
- Perfectionist
- Invisible one
- Possum
- Teacher's pet
- Clown
- Good boy/girl
- Rescuer
- Fixer
- Chameleon
- Diplomat

Think back about the survival strategies you adopted and consider whether they still work for you. If you are still acting as an archetype, you're not living from a place of spontaneity and joy. Your survival strategy, developed in childhood, may have been an effective or even brilliant solution to staying safe and getting love. But ask yourself if it is now actually wreaking havoc in your life. In your journal, write down the problematic ways it affects you. Then ask yourself what other options you may have to be more whole, more complete on your own. Journal about this in depth.

Connecting the Dots

Our emotions and beliefs don't exist in a vacuum but grow out of each other and develop into survival strategies that are often no longer effective. It may help to look at each emotion that you feel difficulty expressing or releasing and examine how it connects with specific entrenched beliefs and strategies. This will help you bring everything you have learned in this chapter together.

PRACTICE: Mapping Your Obstructed State

Respond to each of the following statements or questions by writing in your journal. Begin by choosing a feeling that you are most aware of having trouble expressing and connect the dots to its accompanying beliefs, strategies, and archetype. After you do this for one feeling, go on and examine others in turn. Repeat this practice as many times as you need. Sample responses are in italics.

1. The feeling I am suppressing is: *I feel lonely.*

2. I hold these feelings in what part of my body: *I feel loneliness in my chest.*

3. If your emotions had a size, shape, or color, how would they look or feel? *I feel like there's a big gaping hole in the center of my body.*

4. The beliefs about myself and the world that I have developed from my suppressed emotions are: *I feel lonely because I'm different, I don't fit in, and the world is a cold and harsh place.*

5. The survival strategies I have adopted to get love and stay safe are: *In order to get love, I'm willing to act any way I think will make me more appealing to others. I try to please everyone.*

Explore a New Belief Statement

Now that you see how deep beliefs from your past still rule your life, you can explore fresh options. When you succeed in releasing guilt, or any other destructive feeling, you can enjoy the sensation of being relieved. But since nature abhors a vacuum, you then need to fill the place that carried the guilt. See if you can determine a quality far removed from or opposite of the afflictive emotion you've released. In the case of guilt, I could suggest innocence, which I define as the ability to look at things without preconceptions. As guilt may derive from the belief *I am not enough*, you might also substitute the belief *I am enough just as I am*.

PRACTICE: Filling the Void

Allow your eyes to close and take a few deep breaths. Breathe and feel into the place in your body where you once carried the guilt or other afflictive emotion. Enjoy the comfortable emptiness you've created and revisit a time or situation when you were truly feeling "I am enough." Put the words "I am enough" and the feeling "I am enough" into your belly, or wherever you once felt guilt or another painful emotion. Then put other statements that are new, meaningful beliefs into the void. Do this until you feel filled with possibility. Then open your eyes.

Having unearthed and examined the stored emotions and resulting beliefs and survival strategies from childhood, you are now ready to go deeper into the next layer—to the unconscious aspects of yourself that exist as archetypal repositories from which those emotions, beliefs, and strategies emerged. In the process, you will get to know more of who you are at your core, the essential self that existed before it was obscured by the aftereffects of pain and trauma.

Engage Your Wounded Child and Wonder Child

You can experience a beautiful kind of pure magic when you reconnect with the part of you that is a child, the part filled with playfulness, spontaneity, curiosity, creativity, adventurousness, and even great wisdom. This side of you should never grow up; it should always remain a child. Your child side is closer to your authentic self and your soul essence. In recent years, however, when psychologists have paid attention to what they call the "inner child," they have used the term as a catchall for unresolved childhood traumas and the enduring effects of parental dysfunction that have been stored in the subconscious mind from conception until the onset of puberty. Therapeutic work with the inner child, also called the "child within," was developed by a number of psychologists, including John Bradshaw, who wrote about the ongoing effects of growing up with dysfunctional parents. He believed that a variety of traumatic memories stored in the subconscious from conception to puberty have a profound effect on our behavior later in life. The spiritual teacher Caroline Myss writes at length about what she calls the wounded child archetype, which comes closest to Bradshaw's inner child of several other variants of the child archetype that she examines. It can be easy to view the wounded child as entirely negative, however, and to blame all our troubles on our parents. But we can learn to see our wounded childhood as a source of regeneration and healing. As Myss wrote in her book *Sacred Contracts,* "The painful experiences of the Wounded Child archetype often awaken a deep sense of compassion and a desire to find a path of service aimed at helping other Wounded Children."[3]

It's true that your inner child may have been wounded by traumatic experiences. But a companion archetype, which I call the wonder child, may be far more valuable to you in the long run. The wonder child is the playful, spontaneous, creative, curious, and wise child part that is closer to the authentic you and your soul essence, whereas the wounded child is the aspect of the inner child that was hurt and is in need of care, love, safety, and healing.[4] Although I encourage you to connect most deeply with your wonder child, it is often necessary to work with and heal some aspects of your wounded child before connecting with the wonder child. Even if you suffered severe trauma in childhood, you contain both the wonder child *and* wounded child within you. Our goal is to reparent and heal the wounded child, then reawaken the wonder child.

As you pass from the third layer (emotions) into the fourth layer (inner child), you will encounter and work with both of these aspects of the inner child. Two other resources in the fourth layer will be instrumental in the healing work you will do with your inner child: the adult and the parent. The child, the adult, and the parent are equally important, although most of the work that needs to be done will be with the child self. We cycle through these three different parts throughout the day. Like the legs of a tripod, the three parts need to be balanced to create stability, but they rarely are. When one becomes dominant, we run into difficulties. In this chapter, I will offer you ways to restore the balance among these three parts of your psyche.

Soon after opening her heart, my client Jessica described her first experience with the "Engaging Your Inner Child" practice that you will be doing soon. "I've opened my heart, and at first I feel waves of sadness and some tears, that familiar loneliness. I continue going deeper within, and then there she is! She is about four or five. She is just looking. Her eyes are wide open. She is very excited. She is giddy! I introduce myself to her, and she just laughs and sort of claps her hands. I ask her what she wants to show me or tell me, and she says 'Everything! The universe!' She wants me to go on an adventure with her so she can show me everything in the universe. She is holding her hand out to me. She wants to take me somewhere. She says, 'We are going on an adventure.' She disappears but returns quickly in a safari outfit. She is wearing a pith helmet and is carrying a canteen and a compass. Holding my hand and pulling me, she says, 'Let's go.' She's showing me an even younger me in a yellow bathtub. My mom and my grandma are there. I love my grandma so much. She is like a light. I feel so much love from her. She really gets me without words. She accepts me as I am. I feel so happy! So warm and happy."

The role of the inner child is vastly important, every bit as essential as the inner adult and inner parent, yet it is often overlooked and underrated. Just think of the adult telling the child: "Act your age!" when what the parent really means is "Act *my* age!" The child part of us is the repository of our curiosity and playfulness, and without it, we run the risk of letting our life devolve into a joyless, disciplined drudgery.

The primary role of the adult part is to take on responsibilities, apply logical thinking to solve everyday problems, and make sure the bills are paid on time. It's a bit like the ego, which serves a survival function. Of course, the adult part did not exist when you were a child. The adult part comes into existence over time as we grow and mature. Without the adult part, we would find it difficult to function in the world.

The role of the parental part shares certain adult characteristics but is more of a caretaker and teacher. A good parent is responsible for the ethical and spiritual education of children. The parental part cares for and mentors other people. Ideally, the parent part sees the soul essence within the child part, nurtures it, and invites its qualities to come forward, so to speak.

Reconnect with Your Inner Child

Because we often fail to give the child part of our nature attention, we can lose touch with valuable wisdom and creativity. As a result, we are surprised to make contact with our inner child part as we move deeper inside on the journey to our soul essence. Reconnecting with the inner child is an essential healing step to becoming whole again.

You can think of your inner child in general as a living being who exists within you, comprising both the wonder and wounded child. Parts of the wounded child are stuck in time at certain often difficult or upsetting moments. As we go through life, we experience events that trigger often-unconscious memories of one of those events—which activates our wounded child.

In the last chapter, I encouraged you to examine the strong emotions you feel in any given moment. As they arise, you can also ask yourself what age you seem to be. The first time my wife saw me with my mother, she noticed that I was behaving differently. When my mother served us one of my favorite foods, my inner four-year-old was activated, and I began excitedly clapping my hands. (I'll address how to work with the relative age of your inner child shortly.)

Be a Good Parent so Your Inner Child Can Thrive

You can be the parent that you didn't have or didn't have enough of while growing up. This is known as reparenting yourself. Playing the role of the caretaking, mentoring parent to your own inner child allows you to focus on being a resource for your child and providing healthy parenting that helps the child be more carefree and spontaneous. For example, you may recall the way your grandparents doted on you and seemed to have only loving, supportive things to say—not to mention the dollars they would occasionally slip you—while leaving the discipline to your parents. Assuming that persona with your inner child moves you in the right direction.

As you do the practices in this chapter, think of the three parts—inner child, parent, and adult—as resources that you can draw on as needed. Although it may sound tricky, you need to stay in touch with all three on some level. They can appear with different intensities, but they should all be accessible to you. You need the child's spontaneity, but you also need to balance that carefree attitude with the stabilizing influence of the adult and the guiding wisdom of the parent—the three legs of the tripod I mentioned earlier. Even as you play the role of the carefree child, you can also remember to remain the adult self and be the objective observer. It doesn't help your child for you to act like another child in need of love and attention. The child needs to feel your presence and support as an adult. Likewise, if the inner parent becomes overbearing, you can draw on the adult to keep that part in line and on the child to keep things light. And if the inner adult takes the day off, your parent can maintain order.

As a good parent, above all, you need to keep your inner child safe. As much as you will want to include the inner child in your daily life, there are some activities that are not appropriate for children, even inner children, so you need to exclude the child part specifically. For instance, if you need to have an important meeting with your boss, you don't want to bring your inner child along. You can let the child know that they are free to go off to play at the beach while you take care of business. The same is true, for very different reasons, when engaging in sexual intimacy.

Be alert for adult activities that may trigger the traumas of your wounded child. If you were abused as a child and now need to confront someone in a proactive way, for example, you can tell your child that they do not need to be present. Encourage them to go play in the safe place you established in chapter 1 and promise to reconnect at a later time. The same goes for sexual activity, as dealing with the aftereffects of child sexual abuse is a profound, complex issue. One of the best books on this subject that I recommend is *The Courage to Heal: A Guide for Women Survivors of Child Sexual Abuse,* by Ellen Bass and Laura Davis.[5]

As you engage with your inner child, you will likely make contact with the wounded child. So, as you approach, keep in mind that you need to respect their boundaries—much the way you would if you met a young child at a friend's house or anywhere else. Although you may be moved to embrace your child, you can't assume that your child part wants that or will allow it. From the perspective of the child part, the adult self can appear as just another scary adult that they may be afraid of. You need to first introduce yourself to your child part and ask the child part permission to hold it. I'll guide you through doing this in the coming practices. For now, keep in mind that you will have a very different experience if you contact the seven-year-old who is being shamed by her math teacher compared to if you contact the five-year-old who is playing with a magic wand.

Once you've contacted your child part, you'll want to repeat that experience as often as you can to build trust and confidence. The age of the child will vary from time to time and, as their age changes, they will naturally present different needs and interests. As your relationship develops and deepens, the child usually becomes much more trusting and available, and easier to interact with. And, as the child grows more playful and spontaneous, the wonder child will become more available. You will find it easier to bring the carefree qualities and great wisdom of the wonder child into your everyday life. As you do, you'll establish balance between child self, adult self, and parent self.

The Gifts of Engaging the Wonder Child

As an adult, especially one who has been through trauma, it can be a relief to reconnect with the wonder child, who exhibits fun, spontaneity, creativity, playfulness—and great wisdom. They will exhibit many aspects of the authentic you that you may have forgotten about. This child doesn't just *need* things from us, like love and care, but *offers* surprising healing insights—especially how to make necessary changes in our life. We just need to open our heart to their ideas. Here are some of the gifts you can receive.

- Indeed, the wonder child is close to the creative juice that led the poet Baudelaire to write, "Genius is but childhood rediscovered."[6] Even in the face of traumatic events, the wonder child says, "Let's go draw and paint! Go write that book you've been talking about. Let's find that inspiration within again."

- The wonder child can provide us with insight into how we live—*unfiltered,* since that's the way children communicate as a rule. Curiosity and spontaneity are still active in your child; they haven't yet been adult-erated, as it were.

- It might seem counterintuitive, but the wonder child shares wisdom about relationships from a perspective of love and playfulness, so seek their insight into your romantic partnership or marriage.

- They can help you connect with your deeper wisdom and the inherent curiosity of your soul. Because communication is unfiltered, the wonder child is close to your soul essence and can be a stepping-stone to that core wisdom.

- Connecting with them can help you to gain access to internal guidance rather than looking to another person.

- When you ask your wonder child what they need, their answer is often that they already have what they need. Instead, they may need or want *you* to change or improve some aspect of yourself. They may say, for instance, "You really need a vacation," or "You need to take it easy and have more fun." Their advice is often wise beyond their years, suggesting that you eat better food, not more chips and candy bars, implying that you should not be self-indulgent so much as self-loving.

Keep in mind that you are also likely to trigger or be triggered by the sudden appearance of the wounded child when interacting with the people in your life. If you're speaking with a spouse, partner, close friend, or family member, something you say or do may trigger a memory of a difficult moment in their childhood and activate their wounded child. At that moment, you can ask yourself what the emotional age of the person you are engaged with seems to be. This is not to judge them, but to help you to understand where they're coming from.

If you have children, it's important to heal your relationship with your own inner child, as this will enhance the way you relate to your children. One time when I was taking my two sons to play in the park, they were visibly excited about getting to kick a soccer ball around. But, being the overly responsible adult, I was more focused on keeping track of the time than I was on having fun with them. I realized that I needed to be in touch with my child part to elicit the sense of fun and playfulness that my kids were very much in touch with all the time. When you are planning a fun activity with your kids, it's not a bad idea to pause for a few moments to awaken your inner child. Then you can connect with their sense of playfulness.

Once you make contact with the wonder child, they become easier to consult in the future. If you already have established a working relationship, that's great. But in the likely event that you have become "estranged," know that this strong connection is not only an essential step on the journey to your soul essence; it is also a source of delight.

Seven Steps to Engaging Your Inner Child

You may want to use each of these seven steps individually, although I think you will find that they flow naturally from one to the next. I suggest reading all seven steps once or twice before doing them so you have a sense of their continuity. You will find that you can remain in the relaxed and expanded state of consciousness that you generate in the first step and open your eyes briefly to reread the steps if needed. You can also do these seven practices one or two at a time and then take a break before continuing. If you follow the steps later, or over more than one day, however, it's a good idea to repeat the expanding consciousness practice in step 1 each time you pick up the thread.

The seven steps for working with your inner child are:

1. Connecting

2. Meet and greet

3. Show and tell

4. Holding and loving

5. Power sharing

6. Play time

7. Integration

1. Connecting

Allow your eyes to close and take a few deep, relaxing breaths. Draw the air down into the abdominal area so you can feel your belly expanding as you inhale and contracting slightly as you exhale. Begin the process of relaxing both mind and body, turning inward, and allowing your consciousness to expand beyond the limits of mental mind. Relax your feet and legs; next, relax your hands and arms; relax your neck and shoulders; relax your face, your jaw, your mouth, your eyes, and your forehead.

Imagine yourself in a place where you feel safe, calm, and relaxed. Use all of your senses as vividly as possible to imagine yourself in this special place. See, feel, and experience it. Then, in your imagination, find a spot there where you can either sit or lie down. Intend to go into a deep meditative state of expanded consciousness as you become the objective observer. This gives you a higher perspective that allows you to interact with any or all your inner parts and allows for more flexibility.

Bring your attention to the center of your chest, your heart center. Breathe and feel into the center of your chest, inviting your heart to open, for it is the doorway to your inner world. By diving into your heart center and going deeper within, you will find the younger you. The little one.

Allow yourself to see or sense the younger you right in front of you, whom you can call Little _____ (your name as you prefer it). Notice how this little one appears. Notice what this little one is doing. Notice how this little one is feeling. At this point, all you are doing is observing.

If you have difficulty connecting with the younger you, know that the little one may be hiding. As a result of prior trauma, the younger you may feel so unsafe that they perceive the adult you as just another scary grown-up. Even if you don't initially see or sense the little one there, that one is watching, waiting, and listening to see what you are going to do. Sometimes a little hide-and-seek is going on. Give the child the time they need to come out from hiding.

While it's best to use whatever image of the child comes to you, if you're having difficulty, look at photographs from your childhood if you have them. While looking at a childhood photo of yourself, place your hand on your chest and invite your heart to open. While looking at the expression on your face, your posture, and your position in the photo, notice how the child feels.

If you discover your inner child during a trauma, perform a "rescue" instead of step 2 so you can do an immediate intervention. The introduction can come later. Immediately take the child into your arms and remove them from the abusive or traumatic situation—as you would if you walked into a room and discovered your own child being hurt in any way. Take the child to the "safe place" you established. Once in the safe place, you will need to offer comfort and protect the wounded child from any further harm.

2. Meet and Greet

Introduce yourself to your child part by engaging in an inner dialogue. This is designed to melt the ice and establish communication between you and your inner child. It is the beginning of a true reunion.

> Begin by silently saying something like, "Hi, I'm Big _____ (your first name as you prefer to say it). I have not been there for you, but I am here now, and I'd like to get to know you better." Notice how your inner child responds to you.

After introducing yourself, the child may hide, be silent, or jump into your arms. Savor the moment and avoid telling the child to do anything or say anything. This reunion can be a big deal for both you and your inner child, reaching out across time in a sense, and needs to be engaged with love and respect, allowing the child time and space to receive you as they see fit. How the child self appears to you and interacts with you will be telling.

Often the child has been waiting to connect, and yet, since there has likely been some trauma, they may need something from you. Your child may want to tell you about some experience that they had kept to themselves, either joyful or scary. You may want to take some time connecting with the younger you in this way, or you may want to continue directly into the next step of the practice.

3. Show and Tell

You can follow the meet-and-greet dialogue by moving on to the next stage, which I call "show and tell." Here you can go deeper by asking your child if they want to show or tell you anything of special importance to them. This is a fresh opportunity for your inner child to be seen and heard—something most of us longed for as children. Does the child have a fascination for studying nature or any hobbies or games they like? They may show you an image of symbolic importance to them, and you can ask what it means. They may tell you about a significant event in their life that needs your attention. In some cases, the child is carrying a secret that they haven't shared openly with anyone or they have shared it but weren't heard or believed. If your child part carries such a secret, they will want to share it with their adult self—you.

> See, sense, or imagine before you your child part. You might notice what they're wearing and what age they seem to be. Ask silently, "What do you want to show or tell me?" If your inner child is hesitant, be reassuring. Be open to whatever your inner child presents you with.

4. Holding and Loving Your Child

Here, we do our best to fulfill the child's needs. In this part of this process, you will address any needs or wants that your child expresses. If they need a hug or need love, you can hold them. While holding the little you, you will want to say some of the things the child needed to hear and feel but didn't. These are the things that we have been longing to hear and feel for most of our life.

> Ask the child's permission to hold them; then pick them up and hold them with your arms tight around them, perhaps rocking. While holding

your child tightly, repeat phrases like these over and over, slowly and with feeling:

- You are loved.

- I love you.

- You are safe.

- You are loved, needed, and wanted.

- I'll hold you, and I won't let go.

- Others may come and go, but I'm always here for you.

- It's over. (A child who is stuck in trauma needs to know that.)

- It's not your fault.

- There's nothing you could ever do that would deserve being treated like that.

- You don't have to do anything to earn love. It's your birthright.

- I hold you. I accept you. You are enough just as you are.

- I see you.

Other words and phrases may come to you that you needed to hear as a child and didn't. Feel free to spend some time with your child and see what else comes up for you. A child who has been disappointed by parents will be watching to see if you are going to be like them or if you're going to follow through on your promises.

It's important to follow through. We hear so much about the importance of self-love, but we don't often take the time to practice it. Louise Hay promoted the practice of looking in the mirror and saying, "I love you," or "I approve of myself." Following her advice can have powerful results, but it's even more effective to do this for your child part because it's your child part who needs the love. It's even more direct. Holding your inner child and telling them "I love you" goes directly to the source of the need and fills it.

5. Power Sharing

After you have provided for the child's needs, it's time for a process I call "power sharing." If the child has taken on great responsibility early in life and has been carrying it until now, they have probably been experiencing great anxiety. This is the scared, overburdened child part I encountered in the parking lot of the Rotary Club before my public talk. I was astonished to find that I could liberate his anxiety in less than a minute of connecting. Likewise, Aparna, the physician you may recall from the previous chapter, suffered from similar self-imposed hyper-responsibility. I wish there were more awareness that many cases of anxiety disorder stem from an early dynamic when the child takes on an oversized burden of responsibility. If more therapists realized this, sales of antidepressants and antianxiety medications would plummet.

Power sharing reestablishes the balance of responsibility, caretaking, and playfulness. A practical example might be to tell your child part, "You don't need to have that conversation with my boss. I'll do it, and you can play at the beach." Often, the child is happy to give over that responsibility to the adult self and be playful.

This doesn't imply that we are shirking responsibility; it simply means allowing the different parts of yourself to assume their appropriate roles. The adult takes responsibility and does not expect the child to grow up; instead the child can play. The child should be able to leave the cares and responsibilities to the adults or in this case to the adult self.

I was the oldest of three children whose parents divorced before I was ten. As a young child, I once saw my mother at the kitchen table, crying and really losing it. *Oh no!* I said to myself. *Things are bad enough, but if she falls apart, we'll have no one.* Something in me desperately wanted to comfort my mother, so my survival strategy was to be good, assume responsibility, and make Mom feel better. Part of my inner child healing was not just to make contact with wounded Paul or wonder Paul, but also to have the child who prematurely abandoned playfulness and adopted responsibility and caretaking *give over* that responsibility to my adult self, which of course, didn't exist back then. Now, you can return caretaking to your parental self.

> Holding the child, acknowledge what a remarkable job they've done in surviving as long as they have. "You've handled everything so well, and it's over now. You did it. You don't have to do that anymore. You don't have to be responsible or take are of anyone anymore. I can do that now. I wasn't around back then to do it, but I am here now and can do it. You don't have to. It's over. You're free now, to play. You can run, dance, sing, play. You're free. Free to be yourself."

Even though your child has agreed with your suggestion that you will handle the responsibilities, they may still feel like they must fulfill a certain responsibility at another time because they have done it for years. At this point you can remind them that you've relieved them of that obligation and they can continue to play. This is a direct way of return-ing the balance to the three legs of the tripod consisting of your inner adult, inner child, and inner parent.

6. Now It's Play Time

After meet and greet, show and tell, holding and loving your child, and power sharing, your child part needs some time to play. This is espe-cially true when the child has been forced to take on an adult or care-taker role prematurely and didn't have sufficient time to play during childhood.

If your inner child says something like, "I want to go to the beach," or "Let's go shopping for toys," you can imagine doing that with the child right in this moment, or you may say that you can't do that right now but that you will on the weekend or whenever seems possible. It's important to consider that you'll need to follow through on those promises because otherwise the child will perceive that you're letting them down just like other adults have let them down.

Now you can ask the child, "What do you want to do? Where do you want to go? What would you like to play?" Let your child lead and go explore or play with them.

If you are a parent and your relationship with your inner child is unresolved, your inner child can become resentful and act out when they observe you giving love and attention to your own children. It is even more important to include your inner child when you play with your own children.

7. Integration

An ongoing relationship with your newly awakened inner child is essential. This will require making contact daily. It can be brief and doesn't even need to be an entire practice. But it's important to do this because the child part will be watching and waiting to see if your adult self is going to follow through.

Integration of the aspects of the inner child will occur in several ways. Usually after you gain access to a few different ages and you do some of the above practices, the age of your inner child will stabilize. You will also notice that as the needs of the wounded child part are met, the wounded child becomes less prominent and integrates, while the wonder child becomes more available and more active.

Here is a practice that will give you a way to maintain regular contact with your inner child as you integrate this little one into your daily life and into your whole self.

Take a few deep breaths and place your hand on your chest, your heart center, and connect with the inner child. Imagine holding the inner child again as you did in step 4, holding and loving your child. Now imagine placing the little you there into your heart center. Place your hand over your heart center and remind your child that they are safe, loved, and wanted. Say, "I am here for you." Ask the little one what they need in the moment and what they want to show you and tell you.

Once you have done this, at any time you want, you can take a few breaths, place your hand over your heart center, and check in with your little one. This way you'll find that your child part will become an integral part of your day—and yourself. Your child part will return to becoming a more naturally balanced part of your whole self. You will also gain access to the creative wisdom of the wonder child.

You will not accomplish all of this in one meeting with the inner child; it often takes time for the relationship to develop and requires repetition of the practices. Once you have completed the practices, you can then do them much more briefly with the same benefit.

Supplement this practice by exploring other avenues of communication. I invite you to begin by introducing yourself to the wonder child as above, and then sit with some crayons and draw images that are simple and constructive, like the sun or a smiling face. Bring the child along with you when you're out running errands or just going for a walk in the woods. Imagine your child and continue some of the silent inner dialogues you've been doing here. A powerful way to deepen the relationship is by writing together.

PRACTICE: Writing with Your Child Part

Write to your child from your adult self, using your dominant hand, and then write back from the child to the adult you, using your nondominant hand. This avoids conscious interference. Do write by hand, not on a keyboard. Grab some paper and pencils, crayons, or markers rather than a pen.

Begin by taking a few deep breaths; placing your hand on your chest, your heart center; and connecting with the inner child as you did for integration. Writing with your dominant hand, introduce yourself to your child as you meet and greet them.

Then respond from the child to the adult, using your nondominant hand, sensing what your child feels or wants to say to you.

Then switch hands again and let your adult self write back to your child. Let the dialogue flow organically, until you feel you'd like to take a break. It's better to finish writing whatever comes up for you and then take time to read the dialogue.

Date each conversation and keep them in a section of your journal or a folder. You may be surprised by what you see! When I did this for the first time, I wrote, "I want to try to stay in touch more." And little Paul wrote back, in childlike block printing, "DON'T TRY. DO IT!" On another occasion I wrote, "Little Paul, I love you." He wrote back, "I love you too." That was stunning to me because I focused on taking care of my inner child, but it didn't occur to me that he would return my love. I thought it was a one-way street, but I realized how much my child part loved me. It was such a touching moment that it brought me to tears.

Three Effective Ways of Empowering Yourself

When we are shamed, put down, humiliated, made to feel less than, bullied, abused, or traumatized in any way, we lose some of our power. We are diminished. Now that you have reconnected with your inner child and have completed some essential healing and rebalancing, it is time to reclaim your power.

We begin by defining boundaries and owning our right to say no, then we affirm our right to exist, and finally, we reclaim all the power we have given away to others, in small and large ways, over the course of our life. Here are three practices that you can do in sequence, but you can also do any of them separately at any time that feels appropriate to you.

PRACTICE: Finding Your No

You may have developed the survival strategy of the pleaser and learned to say yes even when it makes you uncomfortable, especially if your boundaries have not been respected. Or, when you say yes, what you really mean is no. Finding your no helps you establish clearer boundaries and is an extremely important aspect of self-care.

If you have difficulty creating boundaries and finding your own personal comfort zone, this practice will help explore why it is difficult to say no and make it easier to draw the line and say no when you need to. Keep in mind that the physical boundary is also a metaphor for the emotional space that other people invade.

You can do this practice with a safe partner whom you trust, and you're going to do it three times. Role-play by having your practice partner pretend to be someone you are uncomfortable around. The first time, your partner will walk toward you. When you feel uncomfortable, you say no, but your partner keeps walking toward you. The second time, your partner will walk toward you. When you feel uncomfortable you will say no, and this time your partner will stop and say, "I hear your no, and I respect it." The third time, your partner will walk toward you. When you feel uncomfortable you will say no. Your partner will stop, turn, and leave the room.

1. As your partner approaches and ignores your no, observe yourself. How long does it take you to say no once you feel discomfort? Is it immediate, or do you override your discomfort and delay saying no? Remain as grounded and present as possible as your practice partner continues to approach. This will let you observe how you respond when your no is ignored. Observe your inner dialogue. Notice what your mental mind is saying to you. You may hear your mental mind saying things like, "I shouldn't be afraid. I shouldn't feel uncomfortable about this. This should be okay"—even though you feel

threatened as the other person comes closer. Then you may hear your mind saying something like, "It will hurt their feelings if I say no; I shouldn't hurt their feelings," as you completely ignore or override your own feelings.

Your partner should come close enough to touch you. As you feel even more uncomfortable, you may find yourself smiling, laughing, or even reaching out for the person you have said no to. This sends a mixed message to the person violating your space that can easily be interpreted as a yes when what you really mean is no. It will be helpful to ask your practice partner to share with you what they observed as you said no and they continued to approach.

2. This time, when, as agreed, your partner stops and says, "I hear you. I respect your no," experience how it feels to have your no heard and respected. Are you comfortable saying no? Do you have any regrets for saying no? Or does it feel good to say no and have your no respected? With practice, your no will come easier!

3. After you say no and your partner stops, turns around, and walks out of the room, observe yourself. This stage often reveals the fear we may have of hurting someone's feelings by asking for what we want as well as the risk of feeling abandoned.

This practice brings awareness, perhaps for the first time, about just how difficult it can be to say no and what some of your fears are around saying no. The most obvious fear is that you may hurt someone's feelings, but the more hidden dynamic may be your fear of being abandoned if you don't give in. Putting others' feelings before your own feelings and safety sets you up for boundary violations and re-wounding.

Your inner child has very good radar for detecting potential danger and unsafe people. When you are feeling uncomfortable and are thinking you should not be feeling that way, check in with your inner child. Place your hand over the center of your chest and silently ask your inner child how they are feeling in the situation or with the individual. Putting your inner child first and taking care of your inner child in these situations will make it easier for you to say no and take care of yourself.

Most of us have had times in our life when we were made to feel like we're not enough. One of the beliefs that is formed as a result of this "feeling less than" is that we don't even have a right to exist. This may manifest as low self-esteem along with the survival strategy to make our self small, invisible, or, as in Marilyn's case, inaudible.

As a young girl, Marilyn had been very lively and spirited, but was constantly shushed by her mother and told to behave, to the point that she became overly quiet and demure and lost a lot of her spunk. As an adult, that manifested as having a very soft voice and great difficulty expressing herself. When she was at one of my workshops, Marilyn spoke very softly in front of the group, and even on a microphone, we could barely make her out at first. She started out weak and when she said, "I have a right to be heard," we still had trouble hearing her! She had come to believe that she didn't even have a right to exist. Working with the "I am" and "I have a right to be" phrases, in the exercises below, was very empowering for her. She kept repeating the phrases until she found her voice. She later wrote to me to say that even just a few weeks later, she had become much better able to express herself, in terms of both speaking up and speaking out. She was astonished at the change.

There are two segments to this practice. Each segment is really a declaration. I think you will find that one will flow naturally into the next. But, if you prefer, you can use them one at a time.

PRACTICE: I Am

"I am" is not a question, and it is not an asking for permission. "I am" is a declaration to yourself, to others, and ultimately to the world! Keep repeating "I am" out loud until it becomes an emphatic statement that feels true to you. You will find that it is most effective to do this standing with feet slightly spread apart.

You can begin by standing with your hand over your belly, eyes closed, and saying out loud, "I AM!" Repeat, "I AM!" a few times as emphatically and with as much confidence as possible. Feel the reverberation of those words in your belly if you can. Once you feel confident with this declaration, remain standing with eyes closed, and imagine telling whomever you need to tell, "I AM!" Once you have told those you need to tell, open your eyes and tell the world, "I AM!"

It may take some time to move the source of the phrase's projection from your head down deeper in the body, into your gut where you can feel it. You can also imagine having your child part by your side and do this together. Give your child permission to join you in saying this out loud. Once you have mastered your "I am," you can personalize it by adding some of the phrases below or creating your own.

- I am.

- I am me.

- I am enough.

- I am okay just as I am.

- I am a woman.

- I am a mother.

- I am a man.

- I am a father.

- I am however I do or don't define my gender and sexuality.

- I am _____.
  (Fill in with your own personal word or phrase.)

PRACTICE: I Have the Right to Be

"I have the right to be" is really an extension of "I am," although many find it more difficult to say with confidence. Whereas "I am" can simply mean I exist, "I have the right to be" is a declaration that not only do I exist, but that I also have the right to exist! Work with "I have the right to be" just as you did with the "I am" declaration until it feels true to you and you can feel it in your gut.

Then imagine turning to someone who made you feel like you didn't have the right to exist—a parent, sibling, bully, abuser, teacher, cleric, boss, commanding officer—and say to that person, "I have the right to be!" Once you have stated clearly and confidently (this may take some time) "I have the right to be," open your eyes and tell the world!

> Start by standing with your feet slightly apart, your eyes closed, and one hand on your solar plexus. Repeat aloud with as much conviction as possible, "I have the right to be!" First tell yourself, then imagine telling others, and finally, open your eyes and tell the world!

Once you can declare "I have the right to be" with confidence and from your gut, you may want to add something more personalized to this declaration. Listed below are some possibilities but feel free to add your own.

- I have the right to exist.

- I have the right to be me.

- I have the right to be alive.

- I have the right to be seen.

- I have the right to be heard.

- I have the right to _____.
  (Fill in with your own personal word or phrase.)

Once you have completed both practices, you will find it empowering to say the declarations together.

"I am! I have the right to be!"

The Soulful Work of Reclaiming Your Power

When someone takes away your power—a parent, a boss, a bully—it's as if they're taking away part of your soul. You may not be aware of it or think of it that way at the time. Sometimes in childhood, we develop the survival strategy of not standing up to our caretakers when they are being abusive because that's the safe thing to do. Our childhood survival strategies were often effective, if not inspired, for getting us through a tough situation, but they no longer serve us in adulthood. Indeed, that brilliant strategy may now actually be wreaking havoc in your life. And so, whatever the original circumstances that led you to develop these survival strategies, you need to reclaim that power and reintegrate it into your body and soul as part of the process of becoming empowered and whole again. Begin by asking yourself these questions.

- Who took away your power? Or rather, who did you give it to?

- Did you learn to give away your power in order to stay safe?

- Did you give away your power hoping to be loved?

- Have you been with someone who was especially good at taking away your power?

- Now turn the equation around and ask yourself: Do I disempower others? Do I take away others' power?

Become conscious that this dynamic can work both ways. It's not uncommon for people who suffer from low self-esteem as a result of letting their power be taken away to turn around and take power from others, just as people who are abused as children often turn into abusers later in life if they don't recognize the pattern. But this does not have to be. Becoming aware of your own tendency to take power from others in this sense can help you avoid feeling like a victim all the time. It's a cyclical dynamic that you can reverse by awakening to how the process works. You will find it much more empowering to take back your power that you have given to others than to take others' power out of fear or anger.

Power is energy. Giving away your power is giving away your energy. Reclaiming your power is actually a form of soul retrieval. In shamanic cultures, the shaman will help a member of the community to regain parts of their soul that they have given away or lost in various ways. Here, you aim to take back those parts of yourself that were taken away or given away so you will become more whole again.

PRACTICE: Call Your Power Back

Prepare for this practice by sitting quietly and recalling a time when you felt disempowered, a time when you gave your power away, it was taken away, or you felt powerless. Invite your inner child to do this practice with you. After all, in many cases it is the child who was made to feel powerless. And the child part can be of great assistance in taking power back.

As part of this practice, you are going to do an energy scan of the person you lost your power to. You will do this with your eyes closed, seeing or sensing your own small energy parts on or around the person you are scanning. Unless you are very intuitive, conducting this scan requires an expanded state of consciousness. So, take more time at the beginning of this practice to achieve the expanded state of consciousness necessary to do the scan and retrieve your power.

Sitting comfortably, allow your eyes to close. Take a few deep letting-go breaths and begin the process of turning inward. Take a few moments to observe your thoughts. Do not engage with them. Just observe them.

Then bring your attention to the center of your chest, your heart center. Breathe and feel into your heart, inviting it to open. Now, imagine yourself in a beautiful, tranquil place. Use all your senses to as vividly as possible imagine being there. Relax both mind and body. When you get the feeling as though you are there, go deeper into a meditative state allowing your consciousness to expand.

Imagine the person to whom (or situation to which) you feel you lost your power as though they are right in front of you. Silently tell them: "I am. I have a right to be. I choose to live."

Using your intuition, scan the individual. As you scan, see or sense bits or pieces of your power on or around them.

Silently or out loud, say to the person who is holding or carrying your power, "I am here to reclaim my power. I gave it to you. You took it from me. It is mine, not yours. I take it back now. You have no right to it. It is mine." And take your power back. Call it back to you.

Breathe it back into your solar plexus. Reclaim it. Take it back. No one has a right to it. It is yours and yours alone.

Welcome back these bits and pieces of yourself. Let them settle back into your body. Let them settle back into your being. Notice how much fuller and more complete you feel.

Tell the one from whom you have reclaimed your power that they can turn to whoever took their power away and do the same thing you just did. They can reclaim their own power back from whoever took it or to whomever they gave it to. In this way you can help end this cycle of disempowerment.

There will most likely be several people or situations from the past for which you will want to repeat this practice. You can continue with them one by one until you feel complete, or simply repeat this practice as you remember situations where you lost your power.

This inner child work is one of the key layers you need to work through on your way to gaining access to your soul essence. You have moved out of your head and into your heart, through the layers of protection, hurts, wounds, and disappointments, overcoming some of the things that were said or done to you and some of the things that you have come to believe of yourself, even though they aren't true. You are reconnecting now with the wisdom and playfulness of the wonder child archetype in you that is more intact, more authentic, moving you even closer to your soul essence.

CHAPTER 5

Integrate the Parts and the Whole You

A college student named Ned was a dedicated bodybuilder. Unfortunately, Ned's dedication and work ethic went to the point of obsession. His father was often critical of him, but his main adversary was his inner critic, who constantly told him, "You're not big enough!" As a result, Ned continually compared himself unfavorably to other bodybuilders. He worked out constantly, pushing too hard and too fast until he finally had a back injury that sidelined him for months—causing him to lose some of the muscle mass and strength he had wanted so much to increase. His inner critic voice had become a kind of self-fulfilling prophecy.

By contrast, his body-building coach was supportive without being critical. "He never criticizes me," Ned said. It occurred to Ned that he would be better off if he could swap his coach for his inner critic. As I guided him through a dialogue with his inner critic, he realized that his critic was leading him to do something that was harmful to his health. He wondered what would happen if he decided to give his inner critic the voice of his coach, using the same repetitive nature but a different text. After trying this approach, Ned found that his inner critic took on a more encouraging voice; it now repeated, "You're doing so well. Keep up the good work!"

Once the subconscious gets on board with adopting a more positive voice, it becomes much easier to achieve what you're trying to do. Positive affirmations made by the conscious mind can be helpful, but by engaging the subconscious in more positive self-talk, you don't have to work so hard to change your behavior.

As Ned's back healed, his attitude improved as well. Feeling less stress, he no longer compared himself to other bodybuilders, and he was able to take a more relaxed approach to working out without losing any of his dedication. Several months later, he had regained his strength and then some. He had also demonstrated a valuable therapeutic principle: our inner critical voices that work against us can be so much more effective when they work with us and for us. These inner voices are often thought of as parts of our psyche.

The Parts of Our Psyche

In the prior chapter, you got in touch with archetypal elements of your subconscious including the wounded child and wonder child. In this chapter, which guides you through the fifth layer of your journey as you dive deeper toward your soul essence, you'll be identifying and engaging with other archetypes and parts of your psyche that drive a wide range of your behaviors. Archetypes have become a source of popular fascination over the past few decades, and with good reason. Briefly put, archetypes are patterns of behavior that all people share to some extent, the significance of which philosophers and psychologists have long explored, from Plato to Carl Jung.

Archetypes can be convenient ways of understanding deeply embedded energy patterns that we share with each other and that are part of our human history. Jung explored the mythology and folklore of the world and discovered patterns of personalities based on common figures, such as the mother, the king, the trickster, as well as general patterns of experience including death, rebirth, and the shadow. Being able to identify specific archetypes can help us clarify the forces that influence our behavior. Some of these archetypes can help us along the way, such as the mother, healer, and wonder child. Others, including the inner critic, saboteur, and victim, can work against us until we learn to make them our allies. While archetypes represent ancient character types that have been with humanity for millennia and are stored in our collective unconscious, many other aspects of your personality are more specific to you.

Another way of looking at the unconscious drivers for our behaviors is to see them as different parts of our personality, or more accurately, our psyche. I find it helpful in doing this work to use the term "psyche," which comes from a Greek root that means "animating spirit," but which can signify the soul or spirit as well as the mind. In some ways, this is a more accurate term because the mind, as most of us conceive it, is much more than just the brain. You don't necessarily have to believe in the "soul" as a theistic concept, but it does help to understand that your consciousness is much vaster than a mechanical brain that thinks logically (some of the time) and an abstract "will" that chooses to act. Psychology, after all, is not the study of the brain but of the mind and spirit that together help us to grow and learn as well as function in the world.

The psyche comprises several parts that may help us or harm us, including the archetypes. In this chapter, I'll introduce what I believe is an especially effective way of working with these aspects of our personality based on a modality commonly known as "parts therapy." Parts therapy is a way of artificially separating out and dialoguing with different parts of your psyche to resolve inner conflict and gain access to inner wisdom.[7]

Once you are out of the thinking mind (layer one) and the heart is open (layer two), you usually experience a rush of emotions (layer three). As these emotions are released, you will find the inner child (layer four). As you have seen, there are primarily two aspects of the inner child that you encountered: the wounded child and the wonder child. As you go deeper within, from layer four to layer five, you will become aware of other significant parts of your psyche that are driving your behavior.

Recognize Your Parts in Action

I realize that when I say you can communicate with different parts of your personality, it may sound like I'm saying that you have two or more of you inside your own head. Actually, there are many. What we call our "self" is a composite of many selves, or parts. By that, I'm not implying anything like the multiple personalities depicted in the popular book and film called *Sybil*.[8] (That condition, now called dissociative identity disorder, is most often the result of a personality shattered by protracted childhood abuse.)

The four most fundamental categories of parts are the physical self, intellectual self, emotional self, and spiritual self. All parts are interrelated, but you will find that each part is more strongly associated with one of these four categories. These parts combine with other aspects to form our composite self. All too often some of these parts are at odds with each other, causing confusion and difficulty. You're probably familiar with the drill: "Part of me really wants to do this, but another part of me is scared to death." And, "I know I can do it, but something inside keeps telling me I can't." Or, "I know this behavior is killing me, but part of me can't live without it." Some therapists refer to parts as "subpersonalities" or "ego states" based on the idea that our psyche is the amalgamation of several distinct people or egos, such as the wounded child or people pleaser. Here I will refer to them all simply as "parts."

We'll begin by identifying the parts that most need your attention and then work on meeting the specific needs of each part. Because these parts are all alive and active within you, once you identify a specific part, you can learn to dialogue with it in much the same way you learned how to dialogue with your inner child.

Looking back at the work you did with your inner child, you will notice that the wounded child is associated with the emotional self and the wonder child is more associated with the spiritual self. As you make progress reparenting and integrating your inner child and continue deeper toward your core self, you will discover other significant parts, each associated with one of these four categories.

You can begin by connecting with the four categories of parts to explore their needs and the insights they have to offer, and then come to a mutual agreement that will bring about healing and empowerment on the deepest levels. In the end, you will be able to transform an unhelpful part and integrate it in a healthful way. Now, let's look at each of the parts in more depth.

Physical self. The physical you, comprising your physical parts, is essentially your body. My client Phil was obviously overweight but was in denial about it. When he entered an expanded state and became the objective observer, he was able to see himself without the rose-colored glasses of his ego. When he did, he saw himself in profile with his sizable belly hanging over his belt. He was horrified. His wife and his doctor had both told him he needed to lose quite a bit of weight, but their words hadn't sunk in. Seeing his physical self, from the perspective of the objective observer, however, had a powerful impact. Phil realized that he indeed needed to lose weight. When he asked his body if there was anything he could do for it, it told him he needed more exercise and to eat better food. It's often much easier to see these things for yourself, once you remove the filter of the ego, than to hear them from someone else.

Intellectual self. In chapter 1, you learned to work with the mental mind by asking it to step aside when you were trying to expand your consciousness and gain access to your heart. Here, you will learn to interact with the intellectual self, which includes mental mind along with other aspects like intellectual curiosity, by personifying it. This will help you explore any inner conflicts you may have with your intellectual self. Several common dynamics are at work in the intellectual self. It often feels that it has to keep a lid on the emotional self because it's afraid that if it lets go of its control of the emotions, everything will come crashing down, and that limits its ability to function rationally as it is designed to do. Moreover, the intellectual self can also get stuck in what I call "trying to make sense of nonsense." You may be struggling to understand how someone could have mistreated you so badly. For instance, how could your sibling walk off with the family heirlooms or the whole inheritance? Why would your best friend steal the guy you were engaged to? As long as your intellectual self is trying to come up with a rational explanation, you are unable to take the necessary actions.

A mother of two young children was feeling depleted and frustrated by devoting virtually all her free time to the care of her children. She loved her kids very much, but she also loved the life of the mind. As she was dialoguing with her mental self, she heard the part exclaiming, "I really need to be able to sit down by myself and read a damn book!" Challenging as it was to find some time in her schedule to engage her intellectual curiosity by reading a good book, she was able to set aside a half-hour before bedtime, when the kids were asleep. She kept two or three books on her nightstand to delve into depending on her mood.

Emotional self. Our emotional parts are the ones that often most need attention, as you likely discovered in working with your stored emotions in chapter 3. Here you will learn to work with the feeling part of yourself by personifying it, as you will with the intellectual self. Your emotional self may appear as a wounded child seeking love and kindness or a wonder child dancing with joy. You may find that as a result of having worked with the wounded child in earlier practices, that part has made progress in healing the emotional aspect of the child. But our emotional parts can appear in a variety of guises.

Sam drank to numb his feelings of loneliness and isolation. It began with a glass of wine to relax after work, but as he had nobody special in his life, he would keep drinking until he fell asleep. When he went into dialogue with his emotional self, he saw it curled up in a little ball. It was feeling all alone and dark. When he asked his emotional self what it needed most, it said that it needed to be held. So, Sam took his emotional self in his arms and held it. At first the self said that it wasn't ready to be held because it was afraid that Sam would leave. Sam told his emotional self that he wouldn't leave, that he just wanted to hold and love it. And once it let him, it felt so good that it wanted to keep on being held. Sam realized that comforting his emotional self was more effective than numbing his feelings of loneliness with alcohol.

Spiritual self. For the most part, we haven't been culturally conditioned to honor and rely on our inner spiritual resources, at least not outside the confines of institutional religion. Some of us indeed feel cut off from our spiritual self and may even think that something is wrong with us if we have difficulty connecting with our spiritual self. But nothing is "wrong" with you; you come equipped with a spiritual self that carries great resources of healing and wisdom, but that may be temporarily obscured from vision, as it were. And so, if you have difficulty making contact with your spiritual self at first, keep in mind that you may need to be patient with yourself and repeat this process.

The spiritual self is a personification of your inner wisdom. It may appear as a sacred being of some kind or just a warm presence that you sense but don't see. You may have read about spiritually transformative experiences that sound mind-blowing, but the most common spiritual experiences are very subtle. They can involve feeling more connected with nature or other people or having a sense of wanting to discover a particular purpose in life rather than just pursuing pleasurable activities.

PRACTICE: Self-Assessment and Integration

This integration exercise is an efficient way to look at and communicate with your four fundamental parts: the physical, intellectual, emotional, and spiritual selves. As you visit each part, take note of its apparent age and condition. Notice in as much detail as possible anything outstanding or unexpected. You can communicate with each part, asking it if it needs attention in any area. You can also ask if the part wishes to communicate anything to the whole.

After recognizing the needs of each of these four parts, you can begin work on getting those needs met. Or, if you have received a helpful insight from one part, you can act on that. Once you have set the healing process in motion, you can bring the four basic parts back together into one composite being. The resulting integration brings greater harmony, balance, and fulfillment into your life.

Allow your eyes to close and take a few deep letting-go breaths, beginning the process of relaxing and turning inward, allowing your consciousness to expand the limits of your mental mind. Take a few moments to observe your thoughts and notice what you hear your mind saying. Now, bring your attention to the center of your chest, your heart center, breathing into it and inviting it to open, for this is the doorway to your inner world. Begin to imagine yourself in a place where you feel very safe, very calm, and very, very relaxed. As you imagine this place as vividly as possible, allow your body to feel as though you are truly there. Allow your consciousness to expand beyond the limits of your mental mind.

In this expanded state, you can see, feel, and experience the various parts or aspects of yourself in an objective way, almost as if you are observing another individual. Take a deep relaxing breath, and allow yourself to see, feel, and experience your physical self. See or sense the physical you.

Notice anything about the physical one that stands out to you. Notice the overall state of health of the physical you. Notice the posture. And what do you notice about the physical you? How is the physical you doing?

Take a moment to silently ask the physical you what it wants to show you or tell you. Make note of what the physical you shows or tells you. Tell the physical you that you get the message. Now, ask the physical you what it needs most currently and make note of this as well. Tell the physical you that you hear what it needs and that you will do what is needed. Now, let the physical you know that you will be back in a few moments.

Take a long slow breath, and let yourself go into a neutral place, relaxing even deeper, maintaining the objective observer state. Now allow yourself to see, feel, and experience the intellectual you. Notice how the intellectual one is doing. And what do you notice? Ask the intellectual one what it wants to show you or tell you and make note of it. Tell the intellectual you that you get the message. Ask the intellectual you what it needs most right now. Tell the intellectual you that you hear what it needs and that you will do what is needed. Now, let the intellectual you know that you will be back in a few moments.

Take a long, slow, deep letting-go breath, and go into a neutral state, maintaining the objective observer. Allow yourself to see, feel, and experience the emotional you. Notice how the emotional you is doing. Does the emotional you appear to be your current age, younger, or older? And what do you notice? Ask the emotional one what it wants to show you or tell you. Tell the emotional one that you get the message. Ask the emotional one what it needs most right now. Take some time to imagine giving the emotional one whatever it needs or tell the emotional one that you hear what it needs and will do what is needed. Let the emotional one know you will return in a few minutes.

Take a nice deep letting-go breath, relaxing even deeper, going into that neutral place again, remaining the objective observer. Now, allow yourself to see, feel, or experience, in whatever form it might appear, your spiritual self. And what do you notice? Take some time to notice how it feels to be in the presence of your spiritual self. Your spiritual self has a message for you. Allow yourself to receive that message now. Perhaps there is something you want to ask your spiritual self. Be open to what it is that your spiritual self shows or tells you in response.

The spiritual self may have a gift that it wants to give you. It may be an energy, it may be words of wisdom, or it may be a tool, object, or symbol. Allow yourself to receive this gift from the spiritual you. If you are unsure what the gift is for or how to use it, ask the spiritual you what you are to do with the gift.

Now bring together all four aspects of yourself that you have visited in the same place. Bring your physical self, your intellectual self, your emotional self, and your spiritual self all together in the same place. Have them stand in a circle holding hands or huddle together with their arms around each other.

Great, now bring them all together into one composite being. Blend them, melt them, bring them together into one. See or sense this new composite being standing tall: strong, healthy, and more alive. Now, become one with that being, and feel the strength, the aliveness, the new sense of health and well-being. Feel the wholeness.

Allow yourself some time to integrate all that you have just experienced. And very gently and gradually begin to return to your normal waking state, grounding and connecting.

Identify the Parts You Need to Work With

Now that you have met and dialogued with the four main parts, you are ready to address a specific issue or topic with the related part. I've found this approach especially useful for anyone who has experienced unresolved trauma and needs help settling internal conflicts. The strength of parts therapy is that it gives you direct access to the parts of your personality whose origin is not always apparent. Not all our internal parts are necessarily helpful, but they all serve a purpose. As we saw with survival strategies that formed in response to certain intolerable situations, a personality part that helped us in childhood may now be causing us problems or even endangering our life. It's important to mention here, however, that one of your parts will never intentionally do anything harmful to you. Even if the part's behavior is causing you harm, its intention is to keep you safe. Ned's inner critic, an aspect of his intellectual self, wanted him to excel at bodybuilding, but its hypercritical approach instead caused him to injure himself.

The good news is that you can interact with each of these parts of your psyche. In most cases, your parts will work for you, but in some circumstances a part may "go rogue" and adopt the critical voice of a teacher, or even a perceived religious figure, such as God or the devil. Or you will find that a part works for itself because it believes that you are incapable of acting on your own behalf. This is often true for the inner critic, to take one example.

Once you have identified the part that's gone rogue, try to find out as much as possible about it. Every part has come to be in your life for some specific purpose. Find out why the part exists by asking its purpose. Find out for whom it works. If the part does not work for you, it may work for Mom or Dad or someone else. All of your parts should be working only for you. If a part does not work for you, it should be released or transformed in some way. Simply remind any rogue part who's the boss.

Dialoguing with Your Parts

As we have seen, traumatic events, especially from childhood, programmed your subconscious mind to act in ways that are sometimes harmful. Merely telling yourself to act in a more constructive way rarely succeeds because that reaches only your conscious mind, which will almost always be overridden by your subconscious. Although the subconscious will not intentionally do you harm, it doesn't always know the best way to *help* you. Parts therapy practices provide you with a way to reprogram your subconscious—not by commanding it to change but by engaging it in the process of changing its approach to helping you. The subconscious is like fertile soil. Any seeds that you—or others—plant in that soil will grow, whether they are helpful or counterproductive. You want to nourish the helpful seeds and transform the harmful ones.

Melanie's habit of overeating for many years had led her to become morbidly obese and diabetic, and she suffered from congestive heart failure. Making matters worse, she had worn through the cartilage in her knees and needed to lose a substantial amount of weight to qualify for knee replacement surgery. When she entered into dialogue with the part of her personality that was causing her to overeat, whom she called Candy Eater, it told her that its purpose was to protect her—from her predatory father, who had begun sexually abusing her at the age of six. The Candy Eater had come into being shortly afterward because, if she ate enough candy and became fat, her father would leave her alone. The strategy eventually succeeded, but over the years, the Candy Eater was still driving her to eat a favorite candy called Dots; now, as a sixty-year-old with diabetes, eating candy was killing her. Melanie had tried behavior modification and every known diet, but she kept gaining back as much or more weight; her father had long since died, but she was still eating candy to keep him away.

Melanie confirmed with the Candy Eater that its job was to keep her safe. Because the subconscious cannot reason, she had to inform the part that eating candy was very dangerous. She asked the Candy Eater if it would help her stop eating candy and start losing weight because that would now keep her safe. It agreed, and over time it helped her lose seventy-five pounds. With the part's unflagging help, Melanie bypassed the step of following a diet or other restrictions. "I don't even go down that aisle in the supermarket anymore," she said regarding the cookie and candy section. "The cookies don't jump off the shelf into my shopping cart anymore!"

By dialoguing with her Candy Eater part, for instance, Melanie went from having her subconscious believe that eating candy would protect her by helping her avoid candy and cookies. But her original, destructive belief was hidden in the dark—in shadow, as Carl Jung put it. Jung described the "shadow" as the part of the psyche that is hidden from the conscious mind because it is not acceptable to us. "The shadow personifies everything that the subject refuses to acknowledge about himself," Jung wrote.[9] The way to assimilate the shadow begins by bringing it into the light and becoming consciously aware of its presence within you. This is true of whichever category the part you are dialoguing with falls into.

Melanie knew that candy and all sweets were deleterious to her health, but she needed to relay that information to her subconscious mind and make it realize that the way to protect her was to help her stop eating sweets and eat only nutritious food.

Making Your Parts into Allies

By using parts therapy, you can get yourself into a relaxed, somewhat expanded state of consciousness and then engage the part of your subconscious that you are working with. Rather than telling it what to do, you will ask it questions, let it respond, and then feed it the information it needs to do what it is designed to do: help and protect you.

That's why it's crucial during this engagement and exploration that you take care not to be judgmental or to alienate the part. Because it's a part of yourself, you don't want to look down on it or get angry at it, but simply find out what it needs. Remember that your subconscious has your best interests at heart and won't do anything to harm you. As you begin to dialogue with your part, it will reveal what's behind that anxiety, anger, or worry (just as in chapter 3 when you allowed your stored emotions to reveal your beliefs and survival strategies).

PRACTICE: Redirecting Your Part

Dialoguing with your parts is a subtle skill, and you may need some practice to get the hang of it. If you're hearing yourself say, *I think...* or *I wonder...*, that's most likely your mental mind speaking to you. You are thinking about it and have probably stepped out of your objective observer mode. When your part communicates directly with you, by contrast, it usually takes the form of images or words, metaphors or symbols. If what you hear the part saying is different from what you thought or expected, you should trust that. Remember that our intention with parts therapy is to bypass the thinking mind and gain access to the subconscious and its deeper wisdom.

Here are the four segments of the practice:

1. Planning your parts session. Identify the issue you want to work on and the part related to that issue. Give the part a fitting title or name, for instance, the Anxious One, the Pizza Eater, or the Angry One.

2. Dialoguing with your part. For this step, you will need to bring yourself into an expanded state of consciousness and become the objective observer. When you begin your dialogue with the part you have named, ask the questions below silently. Make a mental note of the responses or write them down as you go through the practice. Some responses from the part may be nonverbal. The part may show you something or tell you something, such as a scene from the past. It may even react in some other way, such as a gesture or facial expression, in response to your questions. Make a note of anything you notice. Accept any image or other message as something you need to take note of and not dismiss, even if you don't understand its meaning yet.

In the third step of this practice (strategizing a solution), you'll use the answers to your questions to formulate a more effective way of getting your part to help you, so don't be concerned about whether they make sense just yet.

Here are the most relevant questions to ask your part. This is a dynamic process, and you may need to formulate some of your own questions to explore these topics in more detail, depending on how your part responds. Try to be flexible. As we saw with Sam, when he tried to embrace his emotional self, which was curled up in a ball, at first it said it wasn't ready. He needed an intermediate question to move the process along.

- What is your purpose?

- How do you do your job?

- When did you come into my life?

- What made you necessary?

- Who do you work for?

Posing your questions silently and internally to each part is most conducive to maintaining the objective observer state required for parts therapy.

Allow your eyes to close and take a few deep letting-go breaths, beginning the process of relaxing and turning inward and allowing your consciousness to expand beyond the limits of your mental mind. Take a few moments to observe your thoughts and notice what you hear your mind saying. Now, bring your attention to the center of your chest, your heart center, breathing into it and inviting it to open, for this is the doorway to your inner world. Begin to imagine yourself in a place where you feel very safe, very calm, and very, very relaxed. As you imagine this place as vividly as possible, allow your body to feel as though you are truly there.

From your expanded state of consciousness, as the objective observer, allow yourself to see, feel, or experience, in whatever form it might appear, the part that you identified. Imagine it right there in front of you. Notice how it appears and what it seems to be doing. Ask it, "What is your purpose?"

Noticing the part's response, ask, "How do you do your job?" Again, note the response.

Now ask: "When did you come into my life?" Note the response.

"When did you come into my life?" Note the response.

"What made you necessary?" Note the response.

"Who do you work for?" Note the response.

Tell the part you will return soon. Gently and gradually allow yourself to begin to return to your normal waking state, grounding and connecting.

3. Strategizing a solution. Based on the response from your part, you'll need to strategize and take a new course of action. Returning to your normal waking state, write a short sentence that summarizes your part's original role and function based on the answers you received from the part you are working with. Then write a second sentence that will redirect your part to a new, helpful role.

For instance, based on the answers the Candy Eater gave Melanie, she determined that, "He keeps me safe by getting me to eat candy and cookies to get fat—which will make me unattractive." You can distill your strategy sentence into a brief formula; in this case, Melanie could have written, "Eat candy, get fat, stay safe," or simply, "Fat = safe."

Then, reflecting on what you have learned, strategize a more helpful role for your part. Remember that the part won't intentionally harm you, but you do need to provide it with a helpful alternative because it cannot reason for itself. For example, Melanie told the Candy Eater, "Eating candy is actually dangerous and no longer protects me." Then she asked it to help her eat more healthful food.

Because the subconscious cannot reason, we need to give it—spoon-feed it, if you like—any new information it needs to have. Parts can be harmful or helpful—or both, at different times and in different ways. But even though the behavior may be harmful, your parts do not have bad intent. The role of the subconscious mind is to keep us safe and help us survive. For instance, your part might tell you to do something to stay safe. If your subconscious tells you to take a drink, it may be to temporarily relax you. Repeated habitually, of course, all those drinks will eventually cause you harm. That's why you need to negotiate with that part, by informing your subconscious that a particular behavior is harming you. The new understanding that Melanie had to give her part was "Fat = unsafe." So, she created a new role for the Candy Eater: "Avoid eating candy. Lose weight." In effect, Melanie asked the Candy Eater to help her *stop* overeating so she could lose the weight that she no longer needed to protect her; the Candy Eater part would now protect her by helping her eat only nutritious foods.

4. Negotiating an alliance. Once you have strategized a new role for the part, you will take a few moments to reenter the expanded state and engage again with the part. Based on the first sentence you just created above, inform the part why its current behavior is harming rather than helping you. Using the second sentence, ask the part to change its behavior to help you achieve what you want. Recall how Ned, the bodybuilder, got his negative inner critic to adopt the voice of his supportive coach. Occasionally, a part is reluctant to change its role because it is so dedicated to keeping you safe in the only way it has known for many years. In this case you may have to do a little negotiating with your part.

Keep in mind the two sentences you have prepared and start this practice by getting into an expanded state of consciousness and becoming the objective observer.

Allow your eyes to close and take a few deep letting-go breaths, beginning the process of relaxing and turning inward, allowing your consciousness to expand beyond the limits of your mental mind. Take a few moments to observe your thoughts and notice what you hear your mind saying. Now, bring your attention to the center of your chest, your heart center, breathing into it and inviting it to open, for this is the doorway to your inner world. Begin to imagine yourself in a place where you feel very safe, very calm, and very, very relaxed. As you imagine this place as vividly as possible, allow your body to feel as though you are truly there.

Allow yourself to see, feel, or experience, in whatever form it might appear, the part that you identified. Just imagine it in front of you. Use your first sentence to inform the part that the way it has been working to protect you is causing you harm or is no longer necessary. Remind it that it works for you. Using the second sentence you formulated, ask it to help you by doing its job in a new way. Thank it for its willingness to help.

And then gently and gradually allow yourself to begin to return to your normal waking state, grounding and connecting.

While addressing the part, a couple of other common scenarios may come into play. Here I will give you some guidance for working with these situations.

Working with a Part in Need

Often during this work, people discover a part in need of comforting, soothing, and love. As you did with the inner child, you'll want to acknowledge the part, tell it you've heard it, and provide it with what it needs. When Sam's part curled into a ball and said it just needed to be held, that's what he did. It took some negotiating, but his part finally agreed. If you are going to meet the needs of your part, you can either follow through in that moment or, if that's not practicable, negotiate a reasonable time when you can. Say your wounded child wants to play in the sandbox and you have to go back to work, agree that you'll spend time together later that evening or the next free day.

A young man named Martin had been diagnosed with dangerously high cholesterol levels that were contributing to his frequent chest pains and increased risk of heart attack. He was health-conscious, worked out regularly, and took nutritional supplements, but he couldn't seem to control his ice cream fixation. He was eating a pint a day! When Martin dialogued with the part of himself that craved ice cream, he discovered that it was a boy who missed his father. When Martin was growing up, his father worked long hours six days a week and rarely had time for Martin. But on Sundays, his dad would spend some father-and-son time with Martin, which usually involved going out for ice cream. After his father died, Martin got into the habit of eating a pint of ice cream every night, although he had never connected the two events. Whenever he tried to give up ice cream, his subconscious told him that he was taking away his father's love. After further dialogue with his part, Martin determined that he would spend time expressing self-love in ways other than consuming ice cream.

Receiving Insights from Your Part

Recall that your parts, like your inner child, do not only have needs, but often have valuable insights to offer you. For example, Phil's part showed him that he was overweight, and it told him he needed to exercise more and eat more nutritious food. If you encounter that, then acknowledge the insights or wisdom that your part provided. Thank it and then let it know that you intend to take its insights to heart—and follow through by creating a plan to put them into action.

Your Protector Is Likely Holding You Back

The primary job of the protector archetype, as part of our emotional self, is to keep us safe. And yet the strategies we devise to keep ourselves safe, as we have seen, are often ineffective and even counterproductive. I've always been shy and introverted, and my strategy since childhood was to fly under the radar, settling for secondary roles—vice-president, board member—anything so that I wasn't the focus of attention. Not until Michael Newton asked me to help him organize and lead the Newton Institute did I finally have to step up to a clear leadership role. That was a big stretch for me because it went against my protector's strategy.

As time went by, I began to appear on camera and speak to large groups, which was so stressful that I tried to avoid those opportunities. I realized a certain conflict within me. My personality—all those parts I spoke about earlier—makes me laid-back and not particularly ambitious. And yet I'm aware that my soul came into this life with a contract to help other people, specifically by sharing the healing strategies that I developed in response to my own challenges. In taking on a leadership role at the Newton Institute, I learned from Michael that when he spoke about his Life Between Lives regression work, in some areas of the country, he met a lot of resistance. People in the audiences often heckled him, and he even received death threats. I realized that could happen to me as I became more of a public figure in this field, and added to my natural reticence, this knowledge made me hesitate to put myself out in the limelight.

At the same time, I know that we need a protector archetype, but we need it to work *for* us and not against us. Just as you saw with the heart protection in chapter 2, your protector part can often prevent you from feeling what you need to feel. For instance, when your boundaries are repeatedly violated, you need to say no, and your protector needs to help you say no instead of accommodating your abuser, or whoever is harming you. If my protector keeps me safe by avoiding conflict, I finally realized, then I would never learn how to stand up for myself. I needed my protector to step back a bit.

The archetype of the protector is one of our emotional parts that works to keep us safe. The protector can show up as the inner critic, the saboteur, or the victim/perpetrator. So let's take a closer look at these three archetypes.

The Inner Critic

The inner critic is an internalized voice that means to help us do our best, but more often undermines our self-esteem by constantly telling us we're not good enough. It wants us to avoid making mistakes, yet its hypercritical tone can cause us to make the very mistakes it's trying to help us prevent. The inner critic is often associated with perfectionism, demanding that we don't even attempt something unless we can do it to an impossibly high level of faultlessness. By setting the bar too high, it makes it impossible to achieve any level of success and then criticizes us for failing to try hard enough. You would do better to follow the somewhat ironic truism "Anything worth doing is worth doing poorly."

Is the desire for excellence a genuine aspect of your psyche, or do you suspect you've simply internalized the nitpicking of someone else? If you encountered strict teachers—religious or secular—or a parent or coach who was extremely critical and hard-driving, you may have developed your inner critic as a survival tool. "If I do my best," you might have said, "maybe they'll leave me alone or even praise me." On one level, your critic—and the person who modeled it for you—is trying to protect you but may be going about it in the wrong way. It wants you to succeed, perhaps by studying or training harder. Unfortunately, if your critic is constantly harping, it erodes self-esteem to the point where you find it hard to excel. When someone is constantly niggling with you, it's harder to connect with your inner child's creativity and, ultimately, with your soul essence.

PRACTICE: Shrinking Your Inner Critic

If you have an overactive inner critic that is out of control, this practice will help tame it, making it easier to work with. This practice can also be used for someone you know who is critical of you or someone who you feel intimidated by.

Allow your eyes to close and take a few deep relaxing breaths. Imagine your inner critic standing in front of you. You may see or just sense your inner critic's presence. Notice how your inner critic appears. Notice how you feel facing your inner critic.

Now imagine your inner critic growing bigger and bigger, much larger than life, maybe the size of Godzilla! Notice how you feel with your inner critic towering over you.

Then, bring your inner critic back to its original size and notice how you feel.

Now, shrink it down. Shrink it down to the size of a mouse, or an ant, so small that its voice becomes small and squeaky, hilarious, or almost insignificant. And, notice how you feel now.

And now, gently and gradually allow yourself to begin to return to your normal waking state, grounding and connecting.

While the inner critic means well, we need to set it straight. The next practice will help you transform your inner critic using many of the same elements you used in the "Redirecting Your Part" practice above. Remember not to attack your critic because it does have your success at heart, and besides, it will only resist you. As we do with the mental mind when it interferes during a practice, you can thank the critic for its good intentions, but let it know that you would like to establish a different kind of relationship.

After you acknowledge the inner critic and thank it for wanting to help you, you will negotiate a settlement. Your aim here is to get the inner critic at least to back off from its nonstop criticism. An even better solution is to ask the critic to agree to become your inner advocate. If the inner critic can cause so much grief, why not ask it to become a cheerleader instead? Imagine if the same voice that wears you down all the time were now encouraging you!

If your critic seems receptive to your proposal, shake hands on the deal. If it appears to be resisting, ask what its concern is. Address the concern in a creative way, perhaps fashioning an interim agreement. The critic may say that if it doesn't keep pressure on you, you won't do your homework, or eat better, or whatever you need to change. You can offer a trial period of, say, two weeks, during which it will agree to back off and encourage you—and then see how you do without it constantly criticizing your progress.

It's especially helpful to objectify your inner critic by seeing or sensing it right in front of you so you can interact with it. You have likely already spent some time (probably too much) thinking about your inner critic, so now is your opportunity to engage directly with it. You can now move from endlessly thinking about and evaluating your critic's comments to sensing how you *feel* in its presence. And ultimately, you want to move from feeling to knowing—just as earlier in this book you moved out of your head and into your heart, and you will eventually move into the knowing of your soul.

PRACTICE: Converting the Inner Critic
to the Inner Advocate

In this exercise, you will negotiate a settlement with your inner critic, beginning with a few questions. You may even need to formulate some of your own questions to explore these topics in more detail, depending on how your part responds to your questions and negotiations. Try being flexible.

From your expanded state, allow yourself to see, feel, or experience, in whatever form it might appear, your inner critic. Imagine it right there in front of you. Notice how the inner critic appears and what it seems to be doing. Do you feel intimidated or apprehensive?

Ask the inner critic, "What is your purpose?" Make note of the inner critic's response. Ask, "How do you do your job?" Again, note the response.

Now, ask the inner critic, "When did you come into my life?" and "What made you necessary?" Then, ask, "Who do you work for?" And note the response. Inform the inner critic that by constantly criticizing you, it is causing you harm and causing you to make mistakes. Remind the inner critic that it works for you. Tell your inner critic that you want it to back off of the criticism and to start encouraging you. Tell the critic that you want it to do its job in a new way and become your inner advocate (this may require some negotiation). Thank the inner critic/advocate for its willingness to help. And then gently and gradually allow yourself to begin to return to your normal waking state, grounding and connecting.

The Saboteur

We sabotage ourselves in any number of ways, many of them unconscious. People often work hard to achieve a goal, and just as they're about to succeed, they do something that is almost guaranteed to undermine their impending success. And then, when they fail, they express shock and outrage that some external party has caused their downfall. "I worked my butt off to get that promotion," they say to whoever will listen (even if it's only themselves). "Why didn't it work out?"

The most likely answer is that it was your saboteur working in its misguided way to protect you. Let's say that you did work hard to get a better position at your job, and then you learn that one has suddenly opened up and, more amazing still, has been offered to you. You start to hear an inner voice saying, "Now your friends won't like working for you. Nobody really likes the boss." Or, you may not even be aware of an unconscious thought that says, "Now I'll have to give up more of my free time. Do I really want the promotion that much?" Your protector has made a preemptive strike to avoid the pressure it fears you won't be able to handle.

You might also have a subliminal belief that you shouldn't rise higher in life than your parents did. In some cases, a parent may have planted that idea, likely unaware that they were doing so. As you did with the inner critic, make sure that the saboteur is working for you, ask it why it came into your life and how it works, thank it for protecting you, and tell it that it can better protect you in a way that doesn't harm you. Saboteurs are resourceful, after all, and you can ask yours to protect you from sabotaging yourself or being sabotaged by others. As much as our saboteur may work against us, it can also try to sabotage others. This can be hard to acknowledge as it is part of the shadow that is generally not acceptable to our conscious mind. Do we truly feel better when our colleagues don't do well? Apparently, we do. A quotation attributed to the British novelist Somerset Maugham (and many others) goes, "It is not enough to have achieved personal success. One's best friend must also have failed."[10]

By their nature, saboteurs work in the shadows. They detect other people's weaknesses and figure a way to use those soft spots against them. This proves to be an ineffective management strategy, however, because if you undercut the people around you, you ultimately lose their support and put yourself in a weaker position, not a stronger one. What we need to do is to get our saboteur to recognize the strengths of others as well as our own strengths. Saboteurs are often insightful and use their insight to manipulate others; you can direct it to use those same insights to help you—and others—succeed.

The Victim/Perpetrator: Breaking the Cycle

Most of us have experienced being victimized one way or another. As a result, we feel powerless. One way some people react is by becoming a perpetrator themselves. When I was in training to work with victims of childhood sexual abuse, my instructor was working with imprisoned sexual predators, and in my naïveté, I was outraged. I approached her between classes to demand to know how she could justify working with such predators. Her response was, "What do you think happened to *them?*" At the time, the concept hadn't occurred to me. The cliché "Hurt people hurt people" has a lot of truth to it.

Victims become perpetrators and vice versa. In effect, they are opposite sides of the same coin. That's why simply punishing perpetrators does nothing to heal the impulse. Most playground bullies weren't born the way they are. Most likely someone had to make them feel powerless to create their need to dominate other kids. However, psychiatrists assert that some people are born with a genetic predisposition toward aggression and violence, known technically as idiopathic psychosis, which includes conditions such as schizophrenia and is characterized by a lack of empathy. I would take that further and say that some people have what I would call a "soul predisposition" based on past life experiences. This is a complex topic that we'll develop in more depth, beginning in chapter 6, but suffice to say here that there is more to our parts than purely psychological qualities.

The only way to break the victim-perpetrator cycle is to heal the victim that developed the perpetrator part. The same is true of our own inner perpetrator, which was born out of being victimized and feeling powerless. It's easy to have compassion for victims, but it's important that we develop compassion for the perpetrator as well. You will find it easier to locate that compassion if you also acknowledge that you are not condoning their actions, but simply seeing the victim in the perpetrator.

Early in life, some of us developed a victim part to stay safe instead of standing up to the perpetrator. Over time, our desire to be safe at all costs may lead us to become a "professional" victim. *I'll get more sympathy if I'm always the victim,* this line of thinking goes. *People will feel sorry for me.*

The victim part will work overtime to keep us safe and to get the love and attention we need by being a victim. Although that response may have served you early on, you can now learn to reclaim your power. You need to thank the victim part for keeping you safe and getting what you needed, and then inform it that it can help you have your needs met in other ways. This doesn't mean becoming the perpetrator, which is the direct opposite of victim, but instead acknowledging your responsibility and defending yourself and your rights against attack. It can help you have your needs met in other ways. One way, as we saw earlier, is to find your "no" and establish boundaries.

Parts therapy is very deep, integrative work. Be gentle with yourself and give the work that you have done this far some time to settle in. I believe you will find that many of the inner conflicts you have struggled with, knowingly and unknowingly, will be resolved through what you have done. This will help you attain greater inner peace and balance, preparing you for accessing more of the wisdom that lies within you.

CHAPTER 6

Disentangle and Integrate Fragmented Parts of Your Soul

Up to this point you have moved through five layers in the Essential Healing process. You have been working with your inner world in a way that implies the nonmaterial, spiritual nature of the soul. Now, in the sixth layer, you are ready to reach deeper into soul work and explore more directly the intangible sources of pain, trauma, habitual behavior, and afflictive emotions. In this chapter we will address some of the ways in which you can maneuver aspects of your soul that are entangled with other people, including your parents and ancestors. We will also explore ways to regather parts of your soul that you may have temporarily lost along the way.

If all that sounds a bit abstract, perhaps the closest parallel I can offer is the concept of "entanglement," a key element of quantum physics. Physicists have known for some time now that if they separate two photons—elementary particles of light with complementary electrical charges—and change the charge of one photon, the other photon will instantaneously change its charge, no matter how far apart they are. This is true whether they are separated by a few feet or a few light years. It seems at least as likely that psychical energy can be transmitted across correspondingly large distances of time and space. As you will see, you can not only return the baggage of guilt and shame imposed on you by people in your own lifetime—parents, siblings, teachers, classmates— but you can also neutralize and return the energetic charge generated by burdens of guilt or shame initiated generations ago and perhaps in a different country. When you do this, it not only affects you in the present but also releases the soul of your ancestors from that same burden.

I don't pretend to understand quantum physics; indeed, many physicists admit that they don't know how it works, either, but they accept *that* it works. In a similar fashion, I have seen the effects on people of releasing guilt and shame that had been passed on to them by their forebears and of which they had not been consciously aware. I would ask you at least to consider the possibility that we exist in a state of energetic entanglement with other people, our ancestors, and with "lost" parts of our own soul, a concept that we will be working with throughout the chapter.

"What Do I Carry, and for Whom Do I Carry It?"

You are likely aware of carrying your own baggage, including questionable choices and self-defeating actions from earlier in your life. But you are probably less aware of the baggage you carry for other people, including your parents or siblings, teachers, playground bullies, and the like. To delve deeper into this kind of baggage, you can begin by asking yourself the question, "What do I carry, and for whom do I carry it?" In pursuing the answers to that query, I recommend wherever possible that you speak with your living relatives and look through photo albums and other family archives to help you discern whether your family history (including photos of yourself growing up) may provide clues to origins of any low self-regard, residual guilt, anger, depression, shame, or anxiety that you are feeling. Those feelings may come primarily from your childhood—perhaps from an abusive or neglectful parent, a brother who was killed in an accident, or a sister who is in a mental institution.

David, age twenty-five, hoped to become a lawyer, but he found it difficult to focus on his studies because he was depressed and had bouts of intense anger and verbal abusiveness. His outbursts alienated his fiancée, who left him. David's father, Samuel, is an alcoholic who never had a successful career and struggled to run a small convenience store. Samuel's rage, depression, addiction, and financial instability created an environment of uncertainty and emotional instability for David and his siblings.

For years, David believed that his anger was directed at his father for treating him badly and neglecting him. He tried to solve his problems with his father using various forms of therapy, but still experienced depression, anger, and, more recently, suicidal thoughts and even plans. Working through the "Returning the Baggage You Carry" practice, which you'll see shortly, David realized that because of a deep unseen loyalty to his father, he had unconsciously carried his father's own anger for him. To be free of it, David had to return to his father the anger he carried for him and invite his father to return the anger to its source, his grandfather. Probably because of his father's alcoholism, David was unable to discuss his anger dynamic with him. But after returning his anger, David's depression lifted, and he had far fewer angry outbursts.

Just because your parents' lives are stuck in the past, that doesn't mean you are trapped there as well. Once you return any guilt, shame, anger, or other inherited emotions, everything softens, the fog lifts, and you can finally shake loose of the hidden entanglements. You can then step out of the unhealthy loyalty to your parents that leaves you at the mercy of ancestral blockages. For instance, you may no longer agree to carry a parent's low self-esteem and assume that you are "less than" other people. When you were a child, you may have developed a survival technique that says, "If I don't carry this for Daddy, he might not love me." This process can even start in the womb, where the developing fetus is already absorbing anxiety and other troubling emotions from its mother and, by extension, from its father. If you do carry anxiety, moroseness, or depression from your parents, during the next practice, you will learn how you can return it to them so they can also return it to wherever it came from—perhaps their own parents or grandparents.

Nurturing, helpful, loving energy can then flow through you, connecting you to something greater, to Spirit or the Universe. You will shift from feeling victimized—or, conversely, from being an angry aggressor or perpetrator—to maturing into a balanced, compassionate, and loving being. When we shift to understanding something much larger than our own life, we empower ourselves to take responsibility for our actions. Once we realize that our relatives and ancestors did not purposely make mistakes, that they would have acted differently had they known what we know now, forgiveness comes more easily. We come to see that the real lesson behind the limited "story" of life is that our soul continues its learning and growth.

PRACTICE: Returning the Baggage You Carry

In this practice, you will call upon a person for whom you may carry guilt, shame, anger, fear, or another destructive emotion. It could be one of your parents, a child for whom you carry guilt over having divorced their mother, a friend or acquaintance who is gravely ill, a teacher who guilted you, or a partner who shamed you. During the practice, be aware of the reaction of the person to whom you are returning your baggage. You don't need to take responsibility for how they react, but if you sense that they reject it, then leave it at their feet without judgment. It's not up to you to resolve their actions for them; your job is to refuse to carry it any longer.

You can do this practice in any setting, whether in a bedroom or meditation spot or outside in a forest or park. Imagine that the person is standing before you. Be firm as you do this practice. You are not asking the individual to take the baggage; you are telling them that you are giving it back. You can tell the individual that they can return what you have given them to whomever they got it from, but do not take responsibility for what they do with it. Leave it with them and leave it up to them what they do with it. Otherwise you will still be carrying it.

Take a few centering breaths. Imagine the person you have been carrying something for. Face them and say: "As your loyal _____ (daughter, son, friend, etc.), I have carried this _____ (shame, etc.) for you. It is not mine to carry. With love and respect, I now let go of this and return it to you. It is not mine, and I will not continue to own it, carry it, or believe it any longer. I now return this _____ (shame, etc.) to you."

Tell them, "You can do with it what you will. You may even return it to wherever or whomever you got it from. I now move on with my life and career. I choose to _____ (your personal wish for yourself, something that you will now do because you are free from what you have returned)."

Take some time to notice how the person responds as you return it. If they reject it, you can leave it at their feet without being responsible for what they do with it. Your goal is to refuse to carry it any longer.

As you begin returning shame, for instance, you may find that you have taken on or inherited shame from many people over the course of time. If this is the case, you can use this practice multiple times or for more than one individual. The point is to stop carrying what is not yours and to return what you have carried back to its origins.

Laura's boyfriend constantly criticized her for being overweight. Laura felt shamed about her body but continued to overeat, gain more weight, and feel even more ashamed. When she did this practice and returned her shame to her boyfriend, he was reluctant to take the shame back from her. But when she told him that he could return the shame to whomever he got it from, he was much more willing to accept it. As a result of completing the practice, she felt much freer from shame and came to have a more favorable body image. In the end, she lost the weight *and* got rid of the demeaning boyfriend!

End Your Entanglement with Ancestral Trauma

Your forebears' lives have likely shaped your own life in ways that you don't know. Complex chains of ancestral guilt and trauma can reach out from the past to interfere with your current life. In this section, you will extend the work you've been doing with your child and parent archetypes, going back even further than your own birth to your ancestral lineage of several generations or more. To do this, we'll draw on the work that has been done in depth in this area by my wife, Sophia Kramer, an expert in regression therapy and family systems. Sophia helps people heal and integrate parts of their soul that have been fragmented by trauma through a unique process that seeks to reveal and heal unrecognized family dynamics and unconscious entanglements.[11]

Insights and techniques that Sophia developed over years of working with clients have helped me understand the need to go beyond healing the individual to healing our ancestors and the collective. Having experienced interconnectedness and a sense of complete oneness with all things during my near-death experience, I became aware that we have to go beyond our "me/I" consciousness to achieve wholeness, and ancestral healing gives us one way to do that. Whether an ancestor is dead or alive, their soul and remaining consciousness continue to carry their experiences from the past that have great influence on you as an individual and on society.

Together, Sophia and I have presented workshops dealing with our trauma history, and I am indebted to Sophia for helping me to understand this ancestral dynamic. (The practices and client stories in this section all derive directly from her work.) We are not dealing with DNA and other physical inheritances here, but with a kind of spiritual or nonphysical inheritance that has traveled with and been carried by the soul. So, we will need to work on a broader and deeper level than the psychological. For the same reason, you do not need to do these practices with the person with whom you are seeking to resolve an issue or even necessarily let them know what you are doing.

What You Carry for Your Ancestors

Once we get past the immediate layer of trauma, we can reach back to events that are more distant. Residual shame and guilt may derive from a grandmother who lost her baby, a great-grandparent who was displaced or killed in a war or natural catastrophe, or a gay family member who was shunned generations ago.

Sophia and I have worked with people who carry guilt and shame because their grandfather or great-grandfather was a perpetrator in a war or genocide and was in complete denial about the people he killed and the families who suffered as a result. The offspring of such perpetrators deeply believe *I wasn't responsible for my ancestors' atrocities.* But their conscience and their soul believe differently; they unconsciously carry the belief *My grandfather was a horrible person, and he is responsible, so I carry the guilt for him.* This unconscious belief needs to be identified and healed so they can disentangle themselves from the past and be free of its negative influence. Bear in mind, however, that you don't need to find documentary evidence of such historical traumas. The fact that you may be completely unconscious of the events that initiated the lineage of guilt, shame, or other traumatic residue does not diminish the power they hold within you.

Your soul may be unconsciously entangled with an ancestor's or relative's soul and their trauma. It could be said that a part of your soul is carrying and living out some pattern or dynamic that really belongs to someone before you in your family lineage. During one of our annual workshops in Pietrasanta, Italy, Frank wanted to work on his recurring financial losses and numerous business failures. While doing the "Returning the Baggage You Carry" practice, he realized that he unconsciously carried his great-grandfather's guilt and shame from a failed business venture as well as the resentment from the employees whose money he had stolen trying to save that business before escaping to the United States. As a child, Frank had heard some vague family stories about his "crooked" great-grandfather, but he had no idea that he carried the deceit and failure of his ancestor and that this was the source of his own failures. With this return, Frank was able to solve his own struggles and put an end to generations of financial problems.

Review Your Family Stories

Think about any stories or family tales you have heard. Again, you don't need to have proof of these stories or even believe them to be true. What matters is that you have *heard* them or a rumor about them, and they are now part of your conscious awareness or your subconscious mind. You might want to get photos of your ancestors from relatives or from that box in your attic or ask relatives what they know or recall.

Again, even more important than facts and stories about your ancestors is that you trust your guidance and intuitive movements. Don't think about it. Trust what immediately comes up and follow that intuitive movement. If you feel some resistance to doing the exercise, take time to connect to yourself and remember that this feeling is part of the healing process and will pass.

Return the Negatives and Take the Positives

In the practice that follows, you will be working with two essential dynamics. First you will return the destructive emotion, burden, or pattern that you have been carrying on behalf of your parents and ancestors. Then you will take from your forebears, with gratitude, the things that are good for you and your life.

If you feel or know of specific burdens that you have inherited from your ancestors, such as their anxiety, shame, guilt, or depression, then name that specific thing. If you are aware of any patterns, such as leaving or abandonment, betrayal, keeping secrets, or "going crazy," then name these as well. Or, imagine any possible trauma your parents or lineages could have experienced in their own lives depending on where they lived and any local or global crises they survived.

Likewise, be aware of how some of your own positive traits, such as enthusiasm for making music or growing things in your garden, may have originated with your parents or ancestors. These benefits could encompass any skills they have taught you or any aptitudes they may have passed on to you personally, genetically, or culturally—such as artistic or musical ability, technical or academic skill and know-how, athletic or intellectual capacity, an affinity for spiritual practice, or the ability to handle money and finances.

This practice includes four steps. In the first two steps, you will identify and return the baggage you have inherited. In the last two steps, you will follow the return with accepting love and the talents and abilities that will support you. Just as you need to unburden yourself of guilt and shame, you also need to express appreciation and gratitude for positive qualities and capacities you possess by having been born into your family lineage.

PRACTICE: Returning to Your Parents and Ancestors

Be sure to be in a quiet place where you won't be disturbed. Sit in a chair in an upright position or lie down on your back on the floor, sofa, or bed. Center yourself and make sure that you feel calm and safe.

1. Determining the Origins of What You Will Return

Determine the belief system or issue that you have been carrying and want to return. This may be a repetitive pattern or habit or some behaviors you have been doing for a long time without positive outcome. This will help to formulate your issue into a belief statement, as you did in chapter 3.

Veronica's great-grandmother wrote bad checks that undermined her financial standing. Although Veronica had been unaware of this, she ran up massive credit card debt that she had no realistic hope of paying off. She was aware of the consequences but couldn't seem to stop doing it. Veronica identified this dynamic as one she wanted to work on. Her belief statement was *I always spend money that I don't have.*

Your belief statement could begin as something like *I always worry.* Then ask yourself, "What do I worry about?" Make it specific. *I always worry that I won't have enough money, I worry that people won't like me,* or *I worry that I will get sick again.* Trust what arises because your soul will show you what is ready to be released. If you find it difficult to form a belief sentence as described in chapter 3, you can simply name your issue, for example "my anxiety," "my longing," "my guilt," "always picking the wrong partner," "my illness," "my failures," "my money loss," or "my sadness."

Get comfortable sitting or lying down in a quiet place where you won't be disturbed. Take a nice deep letting-go breath and close your eyes to go on your internal journey. When you are ready, imagine your personal special healing room or safe space. Now, enter this place. Breathe gently with open palms turned up. Feel your heart open and be ready to release and to receive. Call your mother and your father into your healing place. Imagine them standing before you. Imagine their ancestors behind each of them. You might also imagine the countries they came from and where their ancestors came from.

When you look at them while thinking of your issue or belief statement, who do you feel responds to or resonates with it? Is it your father and his side of the family or your mother and her side of the family? To which side do you feel most drawn? (For example, your father's father, your paternal grandfather, might pop up in your mind's eye. Do not start thinking about it. Just trust it.)

2. Returning What You Carry

Now, silently or out loud, call your mother or father (depending on which lineage you have identified as the source) by the name you call them (Mom, Mother, Daddy, etc.). Open your heart and, from a higher perspective beyond personality and ego, envision that you connect from soul to soul. Tell them: "As your loyal daughter/son I have carried this _____ (name your issue) for you and those who came before you. I mean you no harm, but it is not for me to continue to carry this. I refuse to own or carry this any longer. I return this _____ (issue) to you with love and respect. You may return it to whomever you carried it for. And they can return it to whomever they carried it for all the way back to its origins. I put an end to this here."

When you suggest to your parents or forebears that they return to those who preceded them whatever issue you are returning to them, do so knowing that it is not your responsibility to control whether your parents and forebears actually return the issue. As mentioned earlier, it is their responsibility to do so; you are the one who makes the change for yourself. However, your change on the chessboard of your family lineage creates a movement that allows others to shift and move, too.

3. Acknowledging Those Who Came Before You and Returning What You Have Inherited

Acknowledge the ones in the lineage to whom you are returning something by saying, "I see you now. I acknowledge you. You are my _____ (name the relation, grandmother, etc.)." Or, if what you see is vague, say: "You are my ancestor." Then say, "With love, I am releasing _____ (name your issue), and I am returning it to you. Whatever caused you this pain, it is over. You can now understand that you can let go of it. Release it and let it be resolved." You might notice how your ancestor releases something. Or, perhaps someone who came before them does the releasing. In your inner picture, step back and observe from an objective position. Let this go now.

Notice what happens. Notice any shifts in how you feel. Notice any sense of your own energy returning to you. Notice any shifts in those you are returning to, any sense of resolution, of things aligning for them. Perhaps even of things returning to their natural order in the family lineage.

Just as grandparents are often more generous and less judging of their grandkids than their parents, you can accept love and generosity from your ancestors that you didn't get from your parents. Maxine, who didn't get love from her father, found through the next part of this practice that although her father was unable to express love openly, she could receive that love from her grandparents. She even felt that her father benefited from this shower of love as he became more loving toward her after she did the practice.

4. Taking What Your Ancestors Have to Offer

Now consider whatever skills, aptitudes, or talents your ancestor may have passed on to you. Imagine yourself acting on that inherited trait and continue: "_____ (name your ancestor), I now take from you, with gratitude, the things that are good for me and my life." If it is difficult to complete this sentence, you might start by saying, "I thank you for whatever as yet undiscovered abilities may reside in me."

Take a deep breath and notice how you feel. Do you feel emotional? Do you feel more complete? Or freer or more excited? Notice what happens between you and your ancestor. Give yourself time to experience and feel and see what happens. Notice what they show or tell you. If you feel complete after the returning-and-taking steps, imagine that you return everything back to the beginning of the problems or issues you might have carried for them. Tell them, "With gratitude, I am taking all the strengthening and nurturing power from you. And with gratitude, I am leaving with you whatever fate belongs to you." Take into yourself what your ancestors have to offer you. And when you are ready, center yourself, and bring yourself back into the here and now, allowing your eyes to open, grounding and connecting yourself.

Personal Soul Loss and Soul Retrieval

Your soul is fluid and is not static or fixed in one spot the way your body is. When your body is developing in the womb, your soul comes and goes, and only over time does it become fully seated or integrated in your body. Further, during your lifetime various traumas may cause the soul or some part of it to leave the body and become stuck or return to its spirit "home." (Michael Newton's research showed that some portion of our soul remains on the other side, in the spirit world, when we incarnate. When part of your soul splits off during a traumatic event, it may "park" itself there until the trauma is resolved.) Without these soul parts, you are incomplete—making it much harder to live fully, fulfill your purpose, and learn life's lessons.

I refer to this as "personal soul loss" because although it is like the kind that results from ancestral traumas, it is also more immediate and often easier to trace. As I was regressing Victor to a near-death experience he had reported, he described the scene as his car skidded on an icy road and headed toward a light pole. Realizing that a huge impact was imminent, he felt his soul energy pull up out of his body to avoid being present as the speeding car slammed into the pole. When emergency crews arrived, Victor hovered above the scene watching as an EMT worked to free his body and resuscitate him. Once his breathing was restored, he felt himself pulled back into his body, but felt some part of him was left behind.

Although we may lose parts of our soul through any number of traumatic events, these aspects of the soul are not destroyed or lost for good. They are either stuck where the trauma occurred, they are held by the perpetrator who took them, or they have returned "home" to spirit where they reside temporarily. Even if we are not consciously aware that we have lost a part of our soul essence, we feel the effects. We are less than fully engaged in all aspects of our life. We feel as though something is missing or that we are not fully here. We might struggle with anxiety and panic without being able to trace the cause.

Trauma and soul loss can result from a serious accident or illness that profoundly affects you or another member of your family. The impact can be such a shock that it splits off a piece of your soul, leaving that soul fragment with a deep-seated fear or anxiety that is locked in at the time it occurred. Years may pass before you are able to make the connection between your current overpowering anxiety and depression and the event that caused it. Like the examples above, this is a form of personal soul loss that became immobilized in time, so this piece of the puzzle remains missing to you until you search for, find, and reintegrate it.

According to the shamanic tradition, which extends back thousands of years in many parts of the globe, the reason that part of our soul essence splits off during a traumatic event is to help us survive the experience by escaping the full impact of the pain. Shamanic cultures refer to this splitting off as "soul loss," for which the shaman will usually perform a practice called "soul retrieval."[12] In my experience, it can seem as if a certain part of your soul separates and becomes stuck in time or space, resulting in a loss of vital force and ongoing feelings of incompleteness, disconnection, illness, or dissociation. As noted, you may not always be aware that you have lost access to a piece of your soul, such as the ability to feel joy and pleasure or even to feel safe in the world. Until you retrieve that part of your soul, you may not be able to fully experience joy, and so, it is equally important to heal the source of your personal trauma and to resolve the soul loss that occurred as a result of the trauma. Trauma work without soul retrieval is incomplete; it leaves an essential piece of the puzzle missing. Soul retrieval is an all-too-often neglected element of trauma resolution. Bringing these missing soul parts back and integrating them will complete and empower you, returning the aspects of your vital force that had been lost.

A coal miner in Canada had a heart attack while working. He later reported that while he was being resuscitated with a defibrillator, he watched the whole scene from above, including his ambulance ride to the hospital and other details common to a near-death experience. Although he was successfully resuscitated, he felt so unconditionally loved in the place he went during his near-death experience that he was unwilling to return and did so only reluctantly. As a result, he never felt complete after the incident and often dissociated. When he did this soul retrieval practice and returned in his mind's eye to the scene of his collapse and "death," he discovered that because his life at the time of the accident was so challenging, he didn't want to go on living. On a medical level, he was doing well with his pacemaker but still felt that part of his soul was missing, and he didn't know how to resolve the trauma. The soul retrieval practice helped him recover the missing parts of his soul, and he felt that he could be more present for his family, whom he loved, than he had been in the past.

PRACTICE: Soul Retrieval from Personal Trauma and Soul Loss

Recall a time when you know you experienced trauma and suspect that you lost some of your soul energy. As part of this practice, you are going to do an energy scan of the person, place, or situation to which you lost your soul part or parts. You will do this with your eyes closed, seeing or sensing your lost soul fragments and calling them back to you. This scan and retrieval require an altered or expanded state of consciousness. Take enough time at the beginning of this practice to achieve the more expanded state of consciousness necessary to do the scan and recover your soul parts.

Sitting comfortably, allow your eyes to close. Take a few deep letting-go breaths and begin the process of turning inward. Take a few moments to observe your thoughts. Do not engage with them. Just observe them. Then bring your attention to the center of your chest, your heart center. Breathe and feel into your heart, inviting it to open. Now, imagine yourself in a beautiful, tranquil place. Use all of your senses to imagine being there as vividly as possible. Relax both mind and body. When you get the feeling that you are there, go deeper into a meditative state, allowing your consciousness to expand.

Recall the situation when your soul loss occurred. Using your intuition, scan the person, place, or situation for your lost soul parts. As you scan, you will see or sense bits and pieces of your soul that have been lost or stuck in time. Call these soul parts back to you. They are yours and no one else's. They will resonate with your other soul parts, so take them back. You can imagine reaching out for them and pulling them back, or you can breathe them into your heart and solar plexus. Call them back. Take them back. Breathe them back. Reclaim them. Welcome back these soul fragments. Give them time to reintegrate. Let them settle back into your body. Let them settle back into your being. Notice how it feels to have these parts of your soul back.

Grounding and centering yourself, feel into your body and become aware of the room around you, opening your eyes when you feel ready.

In instances in which incidents of violent trauma happened over time, you may want to repeat this practice and continue through the incidents one by one until you feel complete. Or, you may repeat this practice later as you remember situations where you lost some of your soul energy and are ready to retrieve it.

A Movement Toward Death

As I was writing this book, I heard from a woman named Rashanna, who had cancer for several years and was told by the oncologists that they could not do anything more for her. They advised her to go home and prepare to enter palliative care. Her husband, Leon, had been taking care of Rashanna every day for two years, but shortly after she returned home, he broke his arm and needed to place her into hospice care. There, the first thing the hospice workers did was to test Rashanna for COVID-19, the coronavirus. When she tested positive, they told Leon that he could not stay with her in hospice but could only visit for an hour at most. They then tested him, and when he, too, was found to have the virus, although he was asymptomatic, the hospice center told him that he could not enter the facility to see his wife—ever again. And so, after nearly two years of caring for her every day, he couldn't be with her as she neared death, a situation that caused them both great anguish.

Leon told me, "I just hope I can die soon and be with her in the afterlife." He said that he would never kill himself, but he still hoped he would die. This is what I call a "movement toward death." This does not mean that you are considering suicide or "assisted dying" as an option, but that, as you entertain the thought of not wanting to be here, some part of your soul begins moving toward death. As the situation progressed and Leon remained asymptomatic, hospice decided to let him stay with his wife for several hours a day. That provided some relief for the couple, but it remains to be seen how he will cope with her death, which is imminent. Leon could benefit from this practice after what seems to be the inevitable loss of Rashanna—after having time to grieve his wife's passing.

When you tell yourself over a long period of time that you want to die, your subconscious mind takes your wish literally, and your body responds by making it happen. So, you do need to counteract that movement toward death or your body will follow through on it. One of my earliest hypnotherapy patients was a woman who was living the life of her dreams. She had met a man whom she not only loved dearly but who was also financially secure enough to fulfill a dream of hers by building a hair salon in their magnificent home. And then, seemingly out of the blue, she was diagnosed with stage-four breast cancer. She had come to me after she got the diagnosis, wanting to know why this terrible thing had happened to her. Through several practices, particularly the inner child regression, she was able to recover deeply buried memories that she had suffered through such a painful childhood that she had frequently felt—and told herself—that the only acceptable way out of her situation was to die. She had wished to die with all the power of a child's desire, although that didn't happen at the time. She went on with her life, and it changed for the better. But all along, her body had been complying with her desperate wish to die until it finally succeeded.

If you are living your life for another; if you have ever been in such physical or emotional pain; or if you felt so sad, angry, or depressed that you wished that your life would just end—or thought about ending it yourself—some part of you began the movement toward death. "I choose to live" is an empowering declaration that you can use to reclaim your life and to make the conscious choice to live it fully.

PRACTICE: I Choose to Live

Do this practice with your eyes open and say, "I choose to live," as emphatically as possible. "I choose to live" is different from "I want to live." "I choose to live" is the declaration of having made a conscious choice to live that reverses a past decision (conscious or unconscious) not to continue.

> Standing with feet slightly apart, eyes open, and hand on your lower belly, declare out loud, "I choose to live!" Once you have stated this clearly and confidently (this may take some time), imagine before you anyone you feel you need to say this to and tell them: "I choose to live!"

Are You Wanting to Die for Someone?

Perhaps you had someone close to you die and you thought, *It should have been me*. When someone close to us is very ill or dies, a part of us can want to go for them or go with them. If we are dying for another, we cannot live our own life fully. Georgina, a woman in her midforties, was struggling with extreme fatigue and several challenging physical conditions. Her overall health was slowly deteriorating with no clear medical diagnosis as to why. When I asked her when her health began to decline, she said, "My health has gotten worse since my sister died in a taxi accident in New York City. We are twins, and I knew the moment it happened! I *felt* it. It was such a shock. I miss her so much. It's just so hard to live without her."

It was natural that Georgina was grieving her sister's death and experiencing some depression, but something more seemed to be going on for her grief to have such an impact on her health. As she went through the soul retrieval practice, Georgina said that she felt that some part of her soul had left with her twin, and she described following her into spirit and staying there with her for a time. Her description was reminiscent of a near-death experience, although it was also significantly different in that she did not go through a life review or encounter a being of light. When I led her through the soul retrieval practice to reclaim the part of her soul that had gone with her sister, Georgina was afraid that she would lose touch with her sister if she brought back that soul part. But in the process, she realized that she needed her missing soul fragment in order to live and that without it, her health would continue to worsen. She had to end her movement toward death. Georgina felt more "alive" after integrating her missing soul fragment and, although she continued to grieve her twin's death, her health gradually improved following this practice.

PRACTICE: Choosing to Live in the Face of Death

You can use this variation on the "I Choose to Live" practice to choose to go on living even as a loved one has passed on.

Sitting comfortably, allow your eyes to close. Take a few deep letting-go breaths and begin the process of turning inward. Take a few moments to observe your thoughts. Then bring your attention to the center of your chest, your heart center. Breathe and feel into your heart, inviting it to open. Now, imagine yourself in a beautiful, tranquil place. Use all your senses to as vividly as possible imagine being there. Relax both mind and body. When you get the feeling as though you are there, go deeper into a meditative state, allowing your consciousness to expand.

Imagine that you are facing the person who has died and say, "Even though you died, I choose to live. Even though it's so hard sometimes, I choose to live." Notice how your loved one responds.

Now, call back to you all the soul parts that followed the person into spirit. You will find that they are still connected to you in some way because they are yours. Take them back. You can imagine reaching out for them and pulling them back, or you can breathe them into your heart and solar plexus. Give them time to reintegrate. Let them settle back into your body. Let them settle back into your being. Notice how it feels to have these parts of your soul back.

Now, tell your body, silently or aloud, "Body, I choose to live. Hear me, body. I choose to live."

Grounding and centering yourself, feel into your body and become aware of the room around you. Open when you feel grounded and complete.

Once you can declare "I choose to live" with confidence and force, look through the following list and see if you want to say other variations of the phrase. Or you can generate one of your own.

- Even though you died, I choose to live.

- Even though it's hard sometimes, I choose to live.

- I choose to live for me.

- I choose to live for me, not you or anyone else.

- I choose to live my life.

- I claim my life.

- I reclaim my life.

- I choose to live my life fully.

A great many personal rewards come from doing ancestral healing and soul retrieval. This deeply transformational work goes far beyond your own individual healing. By regaining the fragments of your soul and reintegrating them, you become a catalyst for healing and reconciliation, not only for your soul, but also for your ancestors or loved ones who are involved in the entanglement. You will find it fulfilling to be the one who starts to locate the missing pieces and is able to change the paradigm on the chessboard of your family and the tribe you belong to.

Having begun to work with more subtle layers of your psyche, you can move on now to explore the often-elusive nature of how your physical body communicates with your soul, and vice versa.

CHAPTER 7

Learn to Rely on Your Inner Wisdom

Entering the seventh layer is all about listening to your inner wisdom. You will begin by listening to your body's wisdom, and then go even deeper inside, where you will engage your wise one within. Each and every cell in your body is full of innate wisdom that is being communicated to you constantly. All you have to do is learn to listen. You will be astonished at what you can learn. Whether physical or emotional in nature, disease in general and pain in particular can be messages that your body is sending you. Listening to these messages and responding to them are essential steps in the healing process. If you let these messages go unheeded, true healing is not possible. No matter what medical treatment you might receive for a condition, your symptoms can worsen or recur somewhere, somehow, until you give them your full attention and "get" what they have to tell you.

This listening and getting to know what is uncomfortable is exactly the opposite of what most of us want to do. Our tendency is to hide, ignore, push away, or numb uncomfortable feelings. Yet, the more we ignore or actively numb a painful place or feeling, the "louder" the body will get. Only by bringing your awareness to the affected area and listening to it can you make healing possible.

Before trying to do anything to the part of your body in need, you must first fully explore it. Get to know it. Ask where the ailment or pain came from. Find out how long the underlying cause of your condition has been there. Ask its purpose because it would not be there if it did not have a purpose. As long as it serves some purpose, it will remain. If you need to have it for some reason, you will not be able to transform it or release it, so ask it why it is there. If your knee is the problem, it might tell you that it hurts because you pushed it too hard playing basketball or skiing. Or, it might say that it was your decision to follow your father into his business instead of going to graduate school to pursue your own passion. Your condition may have a physical cause, like having wrenched your knee, being overweight, or having Lyme disease or arthritis, so you want to get a medical workup to rule out other causes, but it has other components that may reach back to earlier in life, to childhood, or even to time in the womb or a past life. Exploring and listening to the uncomfortable place enables it to let up on the intensity of the message it is sending you, and the symptom will begin to diminish or release. Having conveyed its message, it can now let go.

To begin the healing journey in the practice below, you will allow your consciousness to become just the right size to travel through your body and allow your body's wisdom to guide you right to the source of the problem. I say "the source" because the symptom may be different from the source of the problem. You can trust the body to know.

Some time ago, a friend was experiencing acute neck pain and severe headaches. When I asked her about possible causes, she revealed that she had injured her neck some years before in a serious automobile accident, so I naturally assumed that the source of her pain was her old injury. But, much to my surprise, when her body's wisdom guided her consciousness to the source of the problem, she found herself not in her neck but in her heart. When she engaged in dialogue with her heart center, it told her that she needed to have a good cry because she had been holding onto her grief over her mother's death for more than a year. After her mom died, she carried out all the responsible things she needed to do—selling the house, dealing with the will, helping her siblings cope with the loss—but she had yet to shed a tear. The neck pain resulted from what amounted to her subconsciously shutting off the valve of her emotions by not allowing herself to cry so she could do what she had to do.

In the moment her inner body wisdom revealed that to her, she began to weep uncontrollably, letting go of the tears that she had unconsciously held in for so long. Afterward, her pain was gone. The pioneering English psychiatrist and essayist Henry Maudsley (1835–1918) described this phenomenon eloquently: "The sorrow which has no vent in tears may make other organs weep."[13]

The Birth of the Body Wisdom Process

Up to this point, we have been diving deeper within, from the mind to the heart, gaining awareness of our beliefs and survival strategies, exploring the roles of our archetypes and parts, and acknowledging our generational and ancestral lineages. We have now arrived at the place where we can gain access to a deeper level of our inner wisdom. We often think of wisdom as somehow existing separately from the body—"out there," in our "consciousness." But in fact, wisdom resides within the body. We don't recognize it as such because, as we have just seen, we don't really listen to what it is telling us. Working in this chapter with the Body Wisdom Process and the wise one within, we begin not only to listen but also to dialogue with the wisdom that is inherent within us.

Near the beginning of my professional career as a hypnotherapist, I worked for five years in the office of a doctor who specialized in treating patients with chronic ailments and chronic pain, especially fibromyalgia. I was using traditional suggestive hypnosis and hypnoanesthesia—a long-used technique of achieving pain relief through hypnosis while the patient is awake. Dentists had used hypnoanesthesia successfully over the years to relieve pain during certain procedures, such as minor oral surgery. Using a similar process, I was able to help people get relief from chronic pain as well, but that relief was often short-lived, and they typically returned every few weeks for another pain relief treatment. I also taught them to use hypnoanesthesia themselves, but again, the pain relief was usually either temporary, or the pain simply moved to another part of the body. I was frustrated that my patients received such short-term relief.

In the process, I discovered fibromyalgia patients to be the most difficult group to hypnotize. Having been in pain for so long, they found it hard to relax; many of them had learned to disconnect from their body, so they were already in a kind of self-induced numbness. Searching for ways to lower their pain levels even further, I began to experiment by taking the reverse approach from dissociation. Instead of removing their awareness from the pain, I would encourage the patient to become more present in their body and actually to be more, rather than less, conscious of the pain their body was feeling.

Using this approach, which I call "presence-ing," I showed patients how to enter a relationship with their pain instead of disconnecting and attempting to self-anesthetize. As they began to "feel into" their pain and initiate a dialogue with it, the inner wisdom of their body would often reveal the root cause of their condition, which naturally made it much easier to resolve. From this work, I developed what I now call the Body Wisdom Process.

Although at first this method made some patients more aware of their pain because they were no longer dissociating, as they continued with the approach, they often received remarkable breakthroughs. When patients carry on a dialogue with their body that helps them find a way to heal a particular condition, their first reaction is often either curiosity, puzzlement, or quiet astonishment. Sometimes the relief happens immediately, in which case they don't have time to question the nature of the healing modality, but are simply grateful. Other healings take place over time as the person follows through with their body's advice. Once your body has gotten your attention and as you address the causes of your ailment, it will generally begin to back off.

Your Body Has a Message for You

If our body is constantly sending us valuable information, you may ask why we don't seem to hear it. Many of us pull our energy out of the body where it hurts, like a sore knee or acid stomach, because, understandably, we don't want to feel the pain. We may even be angry and feel betrayed by our body for causing us pain. But if we bring our consciousness into our body and trust that our body has innate wisdom, wisdom that's beyond intellect, and we listen to that wisdom, the body will guide us. The hard part is learning to listen to the body's wisdom.

A tennis pro named Tom had what doctors thought was a growth on his adrenal gland, which they wanted to surgically remove. He didn't believe that he needed surgery and came to me for a second opinion. After he opened a dialogue with his adrenal gland and kidney (to which the adrenal is attached), they told him, "Have the surgery. It will save your life!" He was surprised by the message he received but decided to go ahead with the surgery. When the doctors went in to remove the growth, they discovered a cancerous tumor attached to the adrenal, and they removed both the adrenal and kidney, preventing the cancer from spreading to his body. The body usually perceives any surgery as a kind of invasion and tends to resist it, requiring more anesthesia and necessitating an often-lengthy recovery. In this case, having been included in the process by Tom, his body helped the healing process. His anesthesiologist said she needed only half of the anesthesia that would normally have been used, and Tom was able to leave the hospital much sooner than usual for such a procedure. He also required very little pain medication after the surgery.[14]

Hear It from Within

Once when I was being interviewed for a TV show about healing and the mind, I happened to notice that, although my host was dressed neatly in a suit and tie, he was also wearing slippers. I couldn't help noticing this odd contrast, so I asked about it. He didn't look happy about my asking on camera, but he told me he was suffering from gout and that wearing regular shoes was much too painful. Gout is often associated with the rich lifestyles of the aristocracy in previous centuries, but it remains a serious condition that can sometimes lead to amputation. I asked my host, whom I'll call Michael, if he would allow me to show him a practice that could help him find the underlying cause of his ailment. Somewhat reluctantly, he got into the recliner I have in my office, and I guided him into the Body Wisdom Process, which you'll learn in this chapter. I had him shrink his consciousness down—as we did in "Resetting the Protective Alert Level of your 'Control Panel,'" the practice in chapter 2—and travel into the affected foot so he could dialogue with it. In practice, we let his foot talk to him.

The first thing I explained to Michael was that the source of the pain is not always located where the symptoms manifest. I began by having him ask his foot, "What do you want to tell me?" Michael got a bemused look on his face and said he had received a response but that it was too personal to share on camera. That was understandable, and it wasn't as important for me to know the response as it was for him to hear it. As long as he got the message, that was fine with me. As he continued dialoguing with his foot, he was more willing to share the other things that came to him. One of the first things that his foot told him was, "Stop drinking so much wine."

Gout is a form of arthritis caused by excess uric acid in the bloodstream. When uric acid crystals collect in the joints—classically, the joint in the base of the big toe—it becomes extremely painful. Gout is usually exacerbated by an overly rich diet and too much alcohol. The other thing his foot said was, "Stop eating sweetbreads." Michael liked sweetbreads, the sort of rich delicacy that can cause or aggravate gout. He had been told by a doctor to stay away from those foods and wine, but it didn't register for him. But when his foot told him, "I will heal if you avoid these things and make some lifestyle changes," he took it more seriously. As I've said, it's more compelling when our own body or mind tells us something than when we hear it from a doctor or loved one.

At this point I had him tell his body, "I hear you. I got the message." When we don't listen to the body or suppress what it tells us, it just gets louder. The symptoms will grow worse until we finally listen. So, it is important to acknowledge the body, even thank it for getting our attention. If you have chronic pain, it can be hard to say thank you. We would rather hate it and get rid of it. But if we can talk with it and ask what the message is, we can learn and grow from it and then often we don't need it anymore. That's why we tell the chronic pain, in this case, "Thank you. I got it. You can go now."

PRACTICE: Accessing the Body Wisdom Process

Begin with the understanding that your body is full of wisdom and that you can trust that wisdom to reveal the cause of a symptom and guide you to the source of the trouble. Recall that the site of the pain or dysfunction is not necessarily the same as the location of its source. Keep in mind that in exploring the source of the problem, what you "see" does not have to be anatomically correct. As we saw with Michael, the excruciating pain in his foot derived from a problem with his kidney. Your body's wisdom may communicate with you through different mediums, such as words, images, or metaphors. You may also experience physical sensations, such as feeling a cramp or tingling, or hearing buzzing sounds. Simply imagine what it looks or feels like. Take some time to explore the area.

Then you will ask a series of questions, and after dialoguing with the body in this way, you can refer to one or more of the emotional-release techniques that we practiced in chapter 3 (such as "The Volcano Release," "The Balloon Release," and "Releasing Your Burdens"). If further healing is necessary, take some time to imagine what this area would be like if it were perfectly healthy. Imagine healing the condition in whatever way works for you. You might imagine gluing bones together, plucking out cancer cells, massaging your stuck colon, lubricating joints, sanding down arthritis, cooling inflammation, shrinking pain. Changing strong colors like red or black (most common for pain or disease) to soft pastels like pink or gray has a weakening or easing affect. You might soften a hard object or shrink a huge one. Be creative. Whatever you imagine, your body responds to it as though it's truly happening.

The Body Wisdom Process follows these simple steps:

1. Achieve expanded consciousness.

2. Locate the area in need of healing.

3. Explore it.

4. Discover its purpose or message.

5. Thank it and agree to take action.

6. Finally, release or transform the condition.

You have two ways to use the Body Wisdom Process to explore any condition that you want to work on. You can dialogue with the symptom itself, or you can go to the source of the symptom, which may be in an entirely different place. I've created a separate approach for each way, and most likely one will work better for you. Working with the symptom is more appropriate for an acute condition—one that causes immediate pain, like a sprained ankle. Dialoguing with the *source* of the symptom is more effective for chronic conditions—ones in which pain continues to flare up on a regular basis, like osteoarthritis. You can choose one of the following two practices based on whether your condition is acute or chronic. However, if you're not certain which is more appropriate, I would recommend doing both practices and seeing which works better for you.

Both of these practices benefit from what I would call a gestation period. You need to pace yourself as you go through the following directions. Allow yourself time to stop every so often and wait for the responses rather than pushing yourself to come up with a quick thought. When we started these practices in chapter 1 by going "out of your mind," we left time for transitions to take place, and it's even more important to take your time here. Allow visual, verbal, or other sensory reactions to take shape naturally before moving on to the next part of the practice.

Body Wisdom: Dialoguing with the Symptom

Allow your eyes to close and take a few deep letting-go breaths, beginning the process of relaxing and turning inward, allowing your consciousness to expand. Take a few moments to observe your thoughts and notice what you hear your mind saying. Now, bring your attention to the center of your chest, your heart center, breathing into it and inviting it to open, for this is the doorway to your inner world.

Allow your consciousness to become just the right size to be able to travel in your body. Trusting your body's wisdom, go right to the place where you are feeling discomfort. And be there now. Imagine you can see or feel what is going on in this area. Take some time to explore it. Notice the color, texture, shape, smell, and any sounds. What do you notice?

Now, step back a bit, and you will find that you can communicate with the affected area. You can ask it questions, and it will respond. The response may come as words, a knowing, images, or sensations.

Ask this area what it wants to show or tell you. Notice how it responds. Ask it what its purpose is. Ask it what it needs to heal and how long it will take.

Thank it for getting your attention and tell it you have heard it and that it can go now. Promise it that you will take action to help it heal.

Now imagine how this area would look or feel if it were perfectly healthy. Using healing imagery, release what needs to be released or repair what needs to be repaired.

Allow your consciousness to return to its normal size and gently and gradually begin to feel your feet on the floor. Allow yourself some time to integrate all that you have just experienced. And very gently and gradually begin to return to your normal waking state. Grounding and connecting, allow your eyes to open.

Body Wisdom: Dialoguing with the Source of the Issue

Allow your eyes to close and take a few deep letting-go breaths, beginning the process of relaxing and turning inward, allowing your consciousness to expand. Take a few moments to observe your thoughts and notice what you hear your mind saying. Now, bring your attention to the center of your chest, your heart center, breathing into it and inviting it to open, for this is the doorway to your inner world.

Allow your consciousness to become just the right size to be able to travel in your body. Trusting your body's wisdom to guide you right to the source of the issue, be there now. Imagine you can see or feel what is going on in this area. Once you have located the problem area, take some time to explore it. Notice the color, texture, shape, smell, and any sounds. What do you notice?

Now, step back a bit, and you will find you can communicate with the affected area. You can ask it questions, and it will respond. The response may come as words, a knowing, images, or sensations.

Silently ask the source of your issue what it has to show or tell you. Notice how it responds. What does it show or tell you? Ask the source what its purpose is. Ask it what it needs to heal and how long it might take.

Thank it for getting your attention and tell it you have heard it and that it can go now. Promise it that you will take action to help it heal.

Now, imagine how this area would look or feel if it were perfectly healthy.

Allow your consciousness to return to its normal size and gently and gradually begin to feel your feet on the floor. Allow yourself some time to integrate all that you have just experienced. And very gently and gradually begin to return to your normal waking state. Grounding and connecting, allow your eyes to open.

Remember that you can communicate with your body at any time. All you have to do is stop and listen to what it is telling you. Your body is full of wisdom far beyond your intellect. It has been working hard for a long time to get your attention. Now you know how to listen to it and truly hear what it is telling you. Your body will thank you with better health and helpful insights now that it has gotten your full attention.

What the Mind Thinks Is Different from What the Body Tells You

My first home office had a steep set of stairs leading from the office down to the main floor. One day, going too fast, I pitched forward, and in an effort to stop my fall by grabbing onto the banister, I dislocated my shoulder. A friend who was there helped by yanking on my arm to pop my shoulder back in place, but I later discovered that I had also injured my rotator cuff. Some years afterward, I was having difficulty sleeping because of the pain in that shoulder. I used the Body Wisdom Process technique, and the first thing I noticed was that the pain probably resulted from playing catch with my son that spring. That may have been somewhat true, and it was the logical thing, yet there was a much deeper insight that came from doing the practice. When I listened to my body instead of my mental mind, my shoulder said, "You're overextending yourself. You've been growing your practice, you started a nonprofit, and you started a monthly networking group for alternative practitioners." It continued, "You have to let go of something."

I'm typically not one to start something and fail to follow through, but I decided to cut loose from the monthly networking luncheon and told my body I would do so. In that very moment, my inflamed shoulder stopped hurting. As is likely true for many people, that injured shoulder has served as a kind of barometer. Whenever it acts up, it might be that I slept on it funny, but more likely it's trying to tell me something.

Awaken the Wise One Within

The wise one within embodies the full range of masculine and feminine qualities, including a nonbinary identity. As much as we ideally want to develop a balance of genders, I find it's often easier to do a separate practice for each aspect. You can benefit from doing either the practice you feel drawn to or both.

A good friend who is a licensed social worker did his master's thesis based on his research into a number of male therapists who were raised by single moms. These men seemed to have developed more traditionally feminine aspects, which allowed them, in his opinion, to be better, more empathetic therapists. That makes sense to me. In some Asian spiritual traditions, the yin-yang concept and symbol provide an insightful graphic depiction of the balance of masculine and feminine. Yin represents not just the feminine principle, but also the receptive principle, coolness, darkness, and the moon, while yang represents the masculine principle, the active principle, heat, light, and the sun. In the yin-yang symbol we are all familiar with, the origin of yin (the small dot) already exists within the larger sweep of yang, and vice versa. We all have within us masculine and feminine aspects; one may be more prominent in some people, and other people may determine that neither gender is dominant within them, but we all have some mixture.

Nonetheless, many men have tended to overstress their conventionally defined masculine attributes—aggression, strength, action—and to downplay or ignore the feminine attributes that they share with women, such as receptivity to new ideas and the ability to nurture and comfort others. Social restrictions and stereotypes have militated against both women and men developing their nonbinary nature, and we are now in a time of realignment as we recognize the fluidity of gender.

This realignment can sometimes lead to a kind of overcompensation. For instance, some women have told me that they felt compelled to overemphasize what are often less compassionate, masculine attributes because they had come to believe that they need those qualities to succeed in the business and corporate world. And the same is true of academics, medicine, and the military. Clearly, women need to be empowered to seek and enjoy true equality with men in every area of the workplace, but embracing the dog-eat-dog mentality that has been predominant in the business world will not help businesses treat workers, men and women alike, more compassionately. The hyperaggressive, fiercely competitive attitudes of the male workplace, driven almost entirely by the profit motive, have turned out to be destructive of the social fabric in deeper, more disruptive ways.

Discover the Wise Woman Within

At one workshop, the first to volunteer for this exercise was a woman in her thirties named Betty, who shared a long list of issues troubling her. She had founded what became a huge online business with a man who took advantage of her by pressuring her to do more than her fair share of the work. Betty was married but had no children, so work was her main focus and she drove herself relentlessly. When her business partner criticized her, as he frequently did, she was unable to stand up to him because she was so critical of herself and was afraid that if she spoke out, he wouldn't like her. Even though they were equal partners, she referred to him as her boss. Betty was constantly afraid of not pleasing people and of not being liked. As she put it, "I have to be liked to get what I need." Early in life, she had developed her pleaser part to stay safe, but now it was really causing her trouble. Her need to please and be liked made it hard for her to get her employees to do their jobs properly.

When Betty did the practice and met her wise woman, her wise woman wagged her finger at Betty, criticizing her loudly. Although this is unusual, the wise woman's point was to show Betty that this was precisely what she was doing to herself. "You have to stop criticizing yourself because it's holding you back," she said. As she proceeded with the practice, Betty said, "Now the wise woman is showing herself to me as a kind, compassionate, and very handsome man. Any woman who was with him would feel as if she had won the lottery—as if she were the most beloved person in the world! She wants me to know I am loved and that I am enough! I feel so much compassion from her. She is telling me to have the same compassion for myself. She wants me to get over seeing myself as wrong. Because as long as I see myself as wrong, I will perceive others as criticizing me, especially men! That is why she has transformed into a man. She says that I can continue to be hard on myself, but life will be much more enjoyable if I'm not."

If, as Betty's therapist, I had pointed this out to her, she might have seen it as more criticism. But having come from deep within, in the form of the wise woman, it was much easier for her to hear and to act on.

Some months after the workshop, I received an email from Betty. "I've experienced big shifts this past week as a leader and in my relationship with my business partner," she wrote. "As a leader, I'm finding it easier to delegate and create systems for managing workflows, and I feel like I have authority without worrying about 'repercussions' if people don't like what I have asked them to do. With my boss, I also am feeling more empowered, like I have more of my own ground to stand on because I am far less critical of myself. And I did something I've never done before. This past week, when he started yelling at me for a ridiculous reason, I yelled back. More importantly, I didn't feel guilty afterward, as if I had done something terrible that I needed to apologize for—which is how I would have reacted in the past, that is, if I had ever allowed myself to actually yell like that, which I hadn't. In fact, my throat hurt for a few hours afterward; that's how much I yelled—and it feels good!"

Now, here is the practice that Betty did to connect with her wise woman, which you can use to can gain access to this deeper level of wisdom and power.

PRACTICE: Awakening the Wise Woman Within

You may want to keep your journal at your side to record the messages you receive from your wise woman.

Get comfortable with your feet on the floor or sitting cross-legged. Let your eyes close and bring your attention to your breath. Take longer, deeper, letting-go breaths. Begin the process of turning inward and relaxing mind and body.

Begin to imagine yourself in a place where you feel very safe, very calm, and very, very relaxed. As you imagine this place as vividly as possible, allow your body to feel as though you are truly there.

Go deeper down and deeper within and deeper relaxed. Bring your attention to the center of your chest, your heart center—the center of your feelings, emotions, and love. And invite your heart to open, for this truly is the doorway to your inner world. As you breathe into this more open heart, allow whatever feelings you have been holding here to rise to the surface. You may have been strong, courageous, afraid, worried, loving, scared. Whatever the feelings are, open this heart and allow them to come and allow them to go. It might be laughter. It might be tears. It might be a mix. Just allow it. Heart opening.

Breathing in and out, dive deep into your heart now, through all those layers of protection. Through all those different emotions. Deeper and deeper within. Diving all the way down to your womb, to your hara, to your gut. To that place deep within you, where your wise woman dwells. Make that journey now to your wise woman. For she awaits you!

Allow yourself to see, feel, or experience your wise woman before you now. Notice how she appears to you. Notice how it feels to be in her presence. Welcome her forward or go toward her. Take time to enjoy this reunion.

Your wise woman has a message or messages for you. Be open to receive those messages now. What is it that your wise woman shows or tells you?

Your wise woman has a gift for you. What is it that your wise woman offers you? Receive that gift from your wise woman now. If you are unsure what it is for or how to use it, ask her.

Perhaps you have a question for your wise woman. Ask it now.

Now, approach your wise woman, allow her to approach you, and embrace. As you embrace her and as she embraces you, become one with your wise woman, merge with her, for she is who you truly are. Feel the union. Feel the power, creativity, sensuality, and unconditional love. Feel that sacred female energy awakening within you.

As the awakened wise woman that you are, gently and gradually begin to feel your feet on the floor. Feel the chair, sofa, or floor beneath you, grounding in your body. And when you are ready, let your eyes open once again.

After you've done this practice once, you can go back and ask your wise women for insight or advice during the practice. If you have a specific situation on which you'd like to get some insight, before seeking external advice from a friend or teacher, you can begin to draw on your own inner wisdom resources.

Discover the Wise Man Within

During a Wise Man Within workshop in Istanbul, one man who ran the internet technology division for a large company revealed that his father had belittled him growing up for not being "man enough." Paradoxically, the man feared standing up to his father, so he had given away his personal power all his life, and at first, he appeared diminutive and overly quiet. When it came time to locate his wise man, he not only emerged, but he also confronted the spirit of his father. He stated loudly and forcibly, in a deep, gravelly voice, "I am a man!" By the end of the workshop, both his voice and demeanor had changed for the better, and those changes stayed with him even years later when I saw him at a subsequent workshop.

Male energy often manifests as the strength and self-discipline of the warrior put to peaceful purposes, as when, say, National Guard or military troops help save lives during times of natural calamities, floods, and contagion. Obviously, women now serve in the military and have the qualities of strength and self-discipline, but they have not been viewed positively for owning those qualities. Likewise, men are not generally supported for showing sensitivity. You might find the following practice helpful in gaining access to your masculine energy.

PRACTICE: Awakening the Wise Man Within

You may want to keep your journal at your side to record the messages you receive from your wise man.

Get comfortable, sitting in a chair with your feet on the floor or cross-legged. Let your eyes close and bring your attention to your breath. Take longer, deeper, letting-go breaths. Begin the process of turning inward and relaxing mind and body.

Now, imagine yourself in a place where you feel very safe, very calm, and very, very relaxed. As you imagine this place as vividly as possible, allow your body to feel as though you are truly there.

Going deeper down and deeper within, take a moment to observe your thoughts. Now bring your attention to the center of your chest, your heart center, the center of your feelings, emotions, and love. Invite your heart to open, for this truly is the doorway to your inner world. As you breathe into this more open heart, allow whatever feelings you have been holding here to rise to the surface. Letting them come and letting them go.

Breathing in and out, dive deep into this heart now, through all of those layers of protection. Through all of those different emotions. Deeper and deeper within. Diving all the way down to your hara, to your gut. To that place deep within you, where your wise man dwells. Make that journey now to your wise man. For he awaits you!

Allow yourself to see, feel, or experience your wise man before you now. Notice how he appears to you. Notice how it feels to be in his presence. Welcome him forward or go toward him.

Your wise man has a message or messages for you. Be open to receive those messages now. What is it that your wise man has shown or told you?

Your wise man has a gift for you. What is it that your wise man offers you? Receive that gift from your wise man now. If you are unsure what it is for or how to use it, ask him.

Perhaps you have a question for your wise man. Ask him now.

Now, approach your wise man, allow him to approach you, and embrace. As you embrace him and as he embraces you, become one with your wise man, merge with him, for he is who you truly are. Feel the solid strength, your power, your protective and warrior nature, your courageous and fatherly energy. Feel that sacred masculine energy awakening within you.

As the awakened wise man that you are, gently and gradually begin to feel your feet on the floor. Feel the chair, sofa, cushion, or floor beneath you. Grounding in your body, when you are ready, let your eyes open once again, taking time to integrate your experience.

If you have a specific situation on which you'd like to gain insight, you can do this practice again to draw on your own inner wisdom resources and ask your wise man for insight or advice.

Rita was having a problem with panic attacks resulting from her anxiety over her sexual identity. She had been having relationships with both men and women, but because it was more acceptable at the time for her to be with a man, she had established a relationship with a man. She wanted to be monogamous and honor her relationship with this man, but nonetheless cheated on him—with other women. When Rita went through the wise woman practice, she found that her wise woman was "mummified" and buried deep in the ground. She dug up and unwrapped the mummy, and her wise woman told her that because she had felt so unsafe being a female growing up at home—both her father and stepfather had abused her as a child—she had put away her feminine aspect and overdeveloped her masculine characteristics. This worked so well that although she enjoyed her relationship with her boyfriend and future husband, her masculine self felt the need on occasion to have affairs with other women.

After doing the practice, Rita became more comfortable as a woman in a monogamous relationship with a man, and she eventually married her boyfriend and stopped having affairs. She was able to integrate her masculine and feminine aspects and find balance in life.

Learning to look (and listen) within and to draw on your inherent intuitive abilities can make you more self-reliant, instead of drawing only on your logical ability to weigh all the pros and cons. Logical thinking has its place in decision making, but you may find it helpful also to have access to your intuitive wisdom. It can often feel vague or airy to say that we are consulting our intuition, but in fact the opposite is true. The closer we get to the core of our being, the soul essence that I mentioned at the beginning of this book, the more we can rely on our own inner guidance.

Now that you are learning to connect with the inner wisdom of your feminine and masculine aspects, you are ready to regress back to your soul memories that lie even more deeply concealed than the wise woman and man within. We'll do this in layer eight by drawing on the many years of work I've done with Life Between Lives regression.

CHAPTER 8

Regress to Your Soul Memories

Reliving my near-death experience through a practice of regression, as I described in the introduction, was a life-changing event for me. I knew in that moment that I would have to discover a way to help people have that same kind of profound experience without needing to die, or nearly die. The experience was so powerful that I wanted to share it with the world, but I had no clear idea how to at the time. As you approach your soul essence in this eighth layer, the practices that I've developed will open the door to memories of your time spent in the womb as well as memories of your soul's learning accumulated over previous lifetimes. If that sounds like a lot to expect, I can tell you that it took me a while to realize that I could gain access to those kinds of memories myself. Not long after I had been regressed back through my near-death experience, and had begun my search for ways to replicate that experience, Michael Newton invited me to assist in a training. There I watched him conduct a brilliant variation on past life regression. A psychologist and gifted hypnotherapist, Newton had developed a unique form of regression therapy that allowed him to assist clients in achieving expanded consciousness and recalling a period between their death in a previous life and their rebirth in this life. He saw the mind as having three concentric circles: the conscious mind, the subconscious, and the innermost core, which he called the superconscious mind. He believed the superconscious houses our true identity. "The superconscious may not be a level at all, but the soul itself," he wrote.[15]

Newton's breakthrough occurred when he spontaneously moved a past life regression client into a time following her death in one life and before she was reborn into her next life. In that "between" place, he reported, the souls of his clients were often greeted by loved ones, and some encountered a spirit guide who helped them understand what they had accomplished in previous lifetimes. Once Newton saw what happened during this transitional phase in the soul's existence "between lives on Earth," he intentionally set out to bring people into that stage, a process that he called "Life Between Lives" (now commonly abbreviated as LBL).[16] During some thirty-five years of doing regressions, he worked with about seven thousand patients, keeping detailed notes of his sessions.

Based on those notes, he wrote his breakthrough book *Journey of Souls*, which was published in 1994. From then until his death in 2017, Newton continued exploring and creating a roadmap of what the soul goes through between lives. Being there in the room with Newton when he demonstrated how to take someone back to their time in spirit between incarnations, I felt a different kind of lightning bolt go through me. I realized that he was providing me with the missing link I'd been searching for that would allow me to help others experience something like what I'd felt on the beach when I turned forty and dove through all those layers to discover my soul essence. For the second time in just a few years, my life took a new direction.

The aspect of his work that he was displaying eventually allowed me to help my clients resolve specific problems and issues in their current lives. Conducting thousands of past life and Life Between Lives regressions since then, I witnessed the extraordinary restorative effect that the regression process can have on a wide range of physical, psychological, and emotional conditions, including anxiety, depression, and chronic pain. LBL regression can also help people who have larger questions about why they are in a certain situation in life or about what their life mission is. At the same time, they can reexperience themselves as an immortal spiritual being for whom consciousness continues after the death of the body.

It would be unrealistic, and unfair, for me to attempt to guide you through the full process of an LBL regression, which takes seven to eight hours spread over two days. For one thing, it's an interactive procedure that requires the kind of individual feedback between therapist and client that isn't possible in a book of this nature. I can't even perform an LBL regression for myself after all these years. I believe that past life and Life Between Lives regressions are best guided by a trained regression therapist, but I do feel that you can do a self-guided regression to times earlier in *this* life, which includes your life in the womb, and still experience many of the valuable features and insights that you might gain from a session with a trained therapist. In this and the following chapter, you will learn practices that will facilitate womb regression, identifying your soul purpose, and meeting your spirit guide.

The process of hypnosis in regression therapy opens the doorway to the unconscious mind, not only to locate the origins of our stored emotions, beliefs, and survival strategies, but also to discover talents and abilities from the past. Those memories become as accessible as the conscious memories we carry of things that happened to us earlier in life, from early childhood to last week. We may think that memories are stored in the brain, but the fact is that even neuroscientists don't know exactly where long-term memories are stored. Recent theories suggest that new memories are formed in the hippocampus and later transferred to the frontal cortex. But researchers can provide no proof for either location.[17] In the absence of scientific evidence to the contrary, my experience tells me that traumatic memories lodge in the body and the subconscious mind, and a wide variety of memories are stored in the superconscious mind, or soul, over many lifetimes.

Regression therapy asks the conscious, mental mind to step aside so memories (good or painful) can surface from the subconscious. The process is a little like trying to remember the name of someone you just ran into on the street. You may not be able to remember their name in that moment no matter how hard you try, but half an hour later as you're doing something else, the name comes to you unbidden. That's why we ask the mental mind to sit down to one side and just observe and record so the subconscious is free to be activated during regression. We did the same thing in chapter 1 to get the mental mind to stop blocking our access to the heart and emotions so we could reconnect with our buried feelings. Here, we want to get access to the subconscious and superconscious so we can bring into play deeply buried memories of either pleasant or traumatic events from the past. Once we get used to letting subconscious memories float up into consciousness, it becomes easier over time.

When I do hypnotic regressions, I generally regress people first to their childhood memories. One reason for this is to acclimate people to the process of trusting memories and allowing them to surface, instead of trying to remember or "imagine" what happened. I do this even if the client has come in specifically seeking a past life or LBL regression after having read Newton's books or hearing about past life regression. They often want to have a kind of "out of this world" experience, like a spiritual amusement park ride, but that would be counterproductive. In most cases it's better to look at their current life first and work our way back.

Many people have wonderful memories from earlier in their lives that they have forgotten or buried. So, I begin by inviting them to regress to something pleasant or enjoyable from their childhood. They often go back to a birthday party, an experience of nature, or just quiet moments with a parent, sibling, or friend. They don't necessarily always go right to a pleasant moment, however. When I started this process with a woman who told me that she had been sexually abused by her father and insisted that she had *no* pleasant early memories, she regressed to a scene of her father abusing her. But as we progressed through this memory, she recalled that her uncle had entered the room, saw what was happening, and quickly got her out of there. He rescued her and proceeded to care for her, but she had buried that good memory with all the bad ones—a memory of someone who cared about her and rescued her from her incestuous father. Just that one positive memory unlocked a flood of other memories of happier moments that she had entirely blocked out.

People often worry that regression won't work because it sounds like fantasy. But the simple truth is that we regress spontaneously—and often unconsciously—throughout the day. When I hear the sound of ice cubes clinking in a glass, I spontaneously regress back to a time when I was fourteen or fifteen and I would hear my stepfather preparing to have his first drink of the day. That was my red alert to get ready for the drunken rants and rages that were likely to follow. Likewise, whenever I hear the sound of someone shuffling cards, I go back to a time when I was seven or eight and my parents had friends over to play bridge. That's a pleasant association because my brother and I would be in our pajamas, watching our favorite TV shows, and maybe sneaking candy from the kitchen. In both cases, I'm not merely remembering a time in the past, but entering the mood that I felt during those very different scenarios.

With the next practice, you'll begin by regressing to a pleasant memory from childhood, adolescence, or even last year—before moving on to more complex forms of regression.

PRACTICE: Regression to a Pleasant Memory

This practice is not about *trying* to remember, but simply letting memories come to you. If you don't get any pleasant memories from childhood, you can simply go back to something pleasant from recent days, last month, or a year ago, whatever is enjoyable that floats up for you. Even though the aim is to go to a pleasant memory, you may find yourself drifting into a time that is ambiguous or not so pleasant. If that happens, just take a breath or two and go back to your safe place. Then start over and wait for a pleasant time to float into your memory.

Take a few deep letting-go breaths and allow your eyes to close as you begin the process of relaxing both your mind and your body. Relax your feet and legs. Relax your hands and arms. Relax your face, forehead, eyes, and mouth.

Now, take a few moments to observe your thoughts. Just notice what it is you hear your mind saying to you. Now, bring your attention to your heart center, the center of your feelings and emotions. Breathe into your heart center, inviting it to open, as this is the doorway to your inner world. As your heart opens, notice the feelings that rise to the surface. Let these feelings come and let them go.

Now, imagine yourself in a place where you feel safe and calm and relaxed. It can be an actual or imagined place. Use all of your senses as vividly as possible to imagine being there. Get comfortable sitting or lying there and go into a deep meditative state—a state of expanded consciousness. Allow your consciousness to expand beyond the limits of your mental mind.

Begin to float, to drift back in time, along the timeline of your life. Go back now to some pleasant or enjoyable occasion in childhood, not something that you have to try to remember but something that you allow to float up from your deeper mind. Just let it happen. Trust and allow the scene to unfold. It may be something you see, sense, or feel. Take all the time you need to just enjoy your memories as they come. If you feel playful or carefree, allow those feelings to fill you and know that you can come back to this scene and these feelings anytime you want to.

Hold onto those good feelings and gently and gradually return to the current time and place, the current day and date. Come all the way back. Return to your normal state of awareness. Become aware of your body on the chair, couch, or cushion. And when you are ready, allow your eyes to open and take some time to integrate your experience.

Soul Memories in the Womb

As an introvert, I've often struggled with being in front of an audience, even as that has become an integral part of my work. I needed to resolve the increasing discomfort I felt around doing more public appearances. I realized that in all my regressions, I had completely overlooked something. While I was aware of my purpose in this life, it wasn't until I did a regression to the womb that I engaged in a dialogue between my human personality and my soul. I told my soul that getting up in public was painful, and my soul replied, "That's what you're here for." I asked why I had such a shy personality when I needed just the opposite.

My soul said that my personality is what makes people feel safe opening up to and trusting me because I'm not ego-based or have a need to be famous. For the first time, I saw my introversion as an asset, and from that, I recognized that my soul's personality and my human personality are different for a reason. I now have much less conflict about that difference and have found it easier to help others overcome their own discomfort with having a soul's nature and a human personality. By now, you are probably already having glimpses of your soul nature and observing the difference between that and your human nature. As you continue along this path, you'll realize that the nature you glimpse during spiritual experiences—like regression or going into the expanded states you have experienced in the practices throughout this book—is who you really are. The practices in this chapter represent the next step on that journey of expansion into your soul essence.

As you know, the emotions, beliefs, and survival strategies that we developed in childhood have an impact on our current life. But to say that we developed them in childhood is not the whole story. I have seen that in many cases these elements began their development in the womb, where they also were blended with elements carried over from previous lives into this life by our superconscious mind. (Note: I use the terms "superconscious" and "soul" interchangeably.) Once in the womb, moreover, the soul aspects carried from past lives blend with the developing body and brain of the person they will become, including the thoughts and feelings of the parents, especially the mother.

After birth, the subconscious mind remains relatively unfiltered during the first six years of childhood until the conscious, or mental, mind takes charge more fully. For that reason, the emotional and physical environment of the mother will continue to have a major impact on the development of our emotions, beliefs, and strategies.

Those elements that our soul carried over into the womb (the emotions, beliefs, and strategies) combined with all the wisdom and experience that we have gained across multiple lifetimes are also part of our spiritual development. In the womb, the mind, personality, and brain develop along with the body. Meanwhile, the incoming soul with its intention for what it needs to develop in this life is merging with the body in the womb. There is a free coming and going in the womb during gestation, and that merging continues after birth, a process that, according to some, continues for the first six or seven years of physical life.[18]

And so, as we hypnotically regress further back into our life in the womb, we get closer to the authentic self, to our wise one within, closer to the divine plan we brought with us from our previous life. The more of that wisdom we can gain access to, the better able we are to see our true nature in an unobstructed way. But, during the regression, we also need to perceive how that wisdom interacted with the physical body we are developing and the impact it has on our future life.

Gaining Access to In-Utero Memory

All of your experiences are recorded in your subconscious memory, so you can connect with them through regression. And we know from the work of Michael Newton, Brian Weiss, and others that memories are also recorded in the nonmaterial aspect of who you are, your superconscious, or soul. What we refer to as "in-utero memories" are meaningful because they represent our first glimpse into the nature of the soul—of a consciousness that is not yet fully integrated with the body and, so, not affected for better or worse by the life to come.

In-utero memory also disproves the belief that memories are stored in the brain because the brain is not fully formed in the womb. People can often describe in detail events that happened to their mother while they were still in the womb. A middle-aged woman, Muriel, had a phobia of fire so severe that she couldn't have a candle burning anywhere in her house and wouldn't allow her husband to light a fire in the fireplace. While Muriel was at a dinner party at a friend's home, however, the host lit a fire in the fireplace, causing her to run screaming out of the house. That incident led Muriel to seek treatment, and during regression into the womb, she described watching her mother in their home one night when the oil burner caught fire, the house filled with smoke, and her mother ran into the street yelling for her neighbors to call the fire department. Muriel had no conscious memory of the event, but after the session she called her mother, who confirmed the story. Her mother was startled that her daughter asked about it because the event happened while she was pregnant with Muriel, and she had never related the story to her after her birth. Some months later, Muriel reported her delight when her husband was able to set a fire in their fireplace and she had no adverse reaction.

We store other kinds of memories in-utero too. The womb is also the first point of access for memories that are stored in the soul regarding its purpose for coming into a body. Michael Newton's research with clients who regressed to the time between lives established that the soul is engaged with its guides in a series of prelife planning sessions. During those sessions, his clients reported that they worked collaboratively with their guide or guides to determine their game plan for rebirth, based on what their soul needed to work on in its next lifetime.

Cynthia complained that she felt like something had long been missing in her life. She couldn't put her finger on it, and that was bothering her. She was in a supportive relationship, and her material needs were taken care of, but she couldn't shake the feeling that something was missing. Regressing to childhood, she could already feel that something was absent even when she was still quite young. When she regressed back to the womb, she suddenly said, "I'm not alone. There's someone else here. That can't be!" Cynthia finally exclaimed, "I have a twin!" Then she stopped herself and added, "But I don't have a twin, so it can't be. But that's what's been missing."

She left my office confused and disturbed, not sure whether she was speaking literally or metaphorically. That night, when she contacted her mother and asked if she'd had a twin, her mother broke down in tears. She revealed that one of her two babies had been stillborn, but that she had been so heartbroken that she asked the medical attendants to "take care" of the other baby and never spoke about it again.

People who have had near-death experiences say that they often cannot remember a lot of what they learned during them, especially if they occurred during a cardiac arrest or similarly catastrophic event. Their conscious mind often blocks the entire memory of it, and they can't recall it at all. In addition, the use of anesthesia and sedatives in many cases further disrupts the memory of a near-death experience. I believe that a similar disruption occurs at birth as the soul and body leave the "safe place" of the womb, with its cushion of amniotic fluid. The body-soul complex that is a newborn suddenly has to start breathing for itself, warming itself, and in effect, feeding itself. Michael Newton wrote eloquently about the shock of that emergence from the womb:

> Having this time inside our mother does not mean we are fully prepared for the jarring paroxysm of birth, with blinding hospital lights, having to suddenly breathe air, and being physically handled for the first time. My subjects say if they were to compare the moment of birth with that of death, the physical shock of being born is much greater.[19]

In-Utero Regression for Finding Your Purpose in Life

At birth, our soul leaves not merely the comfort of its mother's womb, but also what had been, prior to rebirth, the embrace of expansive, unconditional love, with the freedom to travel anywhere at will, and has to squeeze itself into a tiny, needy, wailing baby utterly dependent on those around it.

Samantha was a successful psychic reader, but she had begun to question her purpose because she never felt like she was accomplishing enough. Although she was seventy years old, she had enormous energy, more than many forty-year-olds I know, and she lived her life with great urgency. For all that, she felt a nagging sense of there being so much more to do. As she regressed to the womb, she experienced that her soul had enormous energy, and as it observed the tiny fetus from above, it wondered how it could possibly shoehorn all its vast energy into that diminutive body in formation. "I have a lot of work to do," she exclaimed. "I have really big things to accomplish!"

Samantha was dismayed that, given her ambitious life plan, she was not going to be able even to walk or talk for several years. "And diapers?" she asked with a laugh. "You must be kidding me! How am I ever going to do everything I need to get done in this life?" At the same time, she saw that her work as a psychic gave her greatly expanded powers that were not restrained by the limits of human physicality. She gradually came to understand her frustrations and was better able to accept her physical limitations. With that acceptance came the realization that she was accomplishing what she had planned to do, even if it didn't feel as if she were.

We are often astonished at how what is revealed during an in-utero regression supports a life plan of which we have been unaware. In his late thirties, Terry told me that he was troubled and wondering about his purpose in life. When I asked him if he could be more specific, he said that he thought maybe it was time to settle down, even though he wasn't really inclined to. He had never held a job or lived in one place for more than two or three years and hadn't had a serious relationship that lasted more than a year or two, and, so, his friends and family were advising that he settle down and gain some stability. After Terry regressed to the womb, he explored how his soul was feeling then about what he was coming to this planet to do. In the process, he reconnected with the nature of his soul, which was to be an explorer. He remembered that while he was in the womb, his goal had been to have as many different experiences as possible in this lifetime. And although he was at the age when most people normally do settle down, he was right on track to accomplish his soul's mission. Learning this helped him to be more comfortable with his resistance to settling down, at least at this point in his life. If he had gone against his life purpose and tried to settle down prematurely, the results could have been painful indeed.

PRACTICE: Regressing to Your Soul's Purpose

You can gain access to your soul memories and gain insight into your life purpose through self-guided regression to the womb. (In the next chapter, after you have met your guide, you will be able to engage in a life review, as a further way to identify your soul's purpose.)

Take a few deep letting-go breaths and allow your eyes to close as you begin the process of relaxing both your mind and your body. Relax your feet and legs. Relax your hands and arms. Relax your face, forehead, eyes, and mouth.

Take a few moments to observe your thoughts. Notice what you hear your mind saying to you. Now, bring your attention to your heart center, the center of your feelings and emotions. Breathe into your heart center, inviting it to open, as this is the doorway to your inner world. As your heart opens, notice the feelings that rise to the surface. Let these feelings come and let them go.

Essential Healing

Now, imagine yourself in a place where you feel safe, calm, and relaxed. It can be an actual or imagined place. Use all of your senses as vividly as possible to imagine being there. Get comfortable sitting or lying there and go into a deep meditative state—a state of expanded consciousness. Allow your consciousness to expand beyond the limits of your mental mind. Begin to float, to drift back in time, along the timeline of your life.

Travel back in time now, along that timeline of your life. Go back to some pleasant or enjoyable occasion very early in childhood, perhaps even baby time. Just let it happen, drift and float all the way back to something pleasant and enjoyable. Allow the scene to unfold and trust what comes. It may be something you see, sense, or feel. Just allow the memories to unfold. Notice what is going on around you. Notice how you feel.

Take another deep, relaxing breath and continue your journey back in time. Travel back now to that unique time in the womb, somewhere midway in your development. Move into the womb and your developing body. What are the first things you notice? Observe how you feel about coming to be born. What is your sense of why you are coming? Ask your soul why it is coming. Ask your soul what it is hoping to do in the coming life. Ask your soul what it wants to learn during this coming lifetime. Take all the time you need to allow your soul to reveal what its purpose is in coming this time.

With a greater understanding of what you are here to do and remembering all that you have experienced, begin your journey back to this day and date, time and place. Come all of the way back. Reconnect with your body and ground yourself. Breathe deeper again. Move your hands and feet a little. Open your eyes when you are ready.

Take a few minutes to record in your journal what you learned about your life's purpose. Repeating this exercise will help you reconnect with your soul's wisdom and purpose for being here, strengthen your understanding, and add clarity to your perception of what your goal is in this lifetime. It can be easy enough to generalize that your mission here is to learn to love, but that's true for all of us on some level. Ask your soul what aspect of love or what application of love you are here to explore.

How Experiences in the Womb Influence Us

Although the state of mind and physical well-being of our parents can affect the developing fetus in lasting ways, we remain largely unconscious of the root causes of our dysfunction. Anxiety can often be reduced by the "Finding Your Safe Place" practice you learned in chapter 1, but it sometimes isn't enough. The reason for this lack of resolution may be that the root cause of the anxiety happened not in early childhood but in the womb or even before this life. For much the same reason that conventional talk therapy has difficulty addressing traumas implanted in the subconscious during early childhood or in utero, it cannot usually tackle past life traumas carried into this life by the soul.

The developing fetus stores anxiety somewhere in the body, often in the belly or chest. The mother's anxiety can also affect the development of the brain and nervous system. It's not that the mother did anything wrong but that she simply experiences anxiety for whatever reason, and the fetus is in a sense marinating in the soup of anxiety while the incoming soul is taking shape. The anxiety that has been absorbed and stored in the belly of the developing fetus will remain there through adulthood. Indeed, if you had difficulty releasing troubling emotions during the various release practices in chapter 3, you may find the next practice more effective because it goes to a deeper level.

The superconscious and subconscious mind taking shape in the developing fetus generates beliefs from stored emotions, including anxiety, fear, depression, and anger. Beliefs such as *I'm not loved or wanted, I'm too much trouble, It's my fault,* or *There's not enough* take shape, live in our subconscious, and profoundly affect our lives.

One way they do that is by generating survival strategies. The incoming soul of the fetus may seek to comfort the mother, perhaps by sending comforting thoughts or energy. Sometimes the soul will cause the fetus to kick in order to call the mother's attention to the anxiety. Here we have a situation in which the baby is having to calm and soothe its mother instead of the other way around. The potential repercussions of that strategy are carried into adult life.

Another strategy—hunkering down—consists of various ways of sheltering the soul by building layers of protective shielding. Yet another strategy leads the developing consciousness of the baby to contract, much like those insects that we called roly-poly bugs that roll into a defensive ball when touched. If the situation in the womb is too uncomfortable, the soul may leave for a time; it may move in and out of the developing body and return only at birth. This can cause problems later in life in terms of your relationship to your body, resulting in disassociation. Even a minor event can trigger the response of leaving the body. Most psychologists don't think of disassociation as soul energy leaving the body, but that is what's happening.

We may also develop limiting beliefs based on events experienced in the womb. Sandy was having great difficulty in her relationship, even though her boyfriend often told her how much he loved her. "He says it, but I can't believe it," she said. "I'm unlovable, so nobody could love me."

When Sandy regressed back to the source of her unlovability, she recalled being in the womb of her sixteen-year-old mother and feeling unloved and unwanted. Her mother, a Catholic, had been sent off to a group home where Catholic parents often sent their unmarried pregnant daughters to have their babies, which they subsequently gave up for adoption. Although Sandy's mother chose not to abort the fetus and gave birth to a healthy girl, during her pregnancy she had neither felt nor expressed love and affection for the life taking shape within her. Once Sandy was born, her mother never held or bonded with her before Sandy was given to another couple. That absence of love, which manifested as indifference, had communicated to Sandy that she was not wanted.

In the womb regression practice, Sandy took herself as a fetus from her mother's womb and placed it in her own womb and told the embryo that she loved and wanted her. She stroked her own belly lovingly as she had seen so many pregnant mothers do. Sandy resolved her feeling of being unlovable by sending the love to the developing baby that it had never received. Following this practice, Sandy discovered that she was able to trust her boyfriend's love, and eventually she married him and started a family of her own.

You have within you the ability to refocus your current life by taking the role of parent on yourself. We often wonder in frustration how we could have chosen our birth parents, but whatever your belief about pre-incarnation planning may be, you certainly have the power to revisit and take charge of your own gestation now. By providing your fetus with the love and comfort it didn't receive, by releasing the causes of anxiety or fear that affected your mother and hence you yourself, you can in a sense become the parent you wish you had had.

PRACTICE: Reparenting Your In-Utero Self

In this practice you will begin by regressing yourself back through childhood into the womb. Once there, you will take the fetus and place it in your heart or womb and release any afflictive emotions that came from your mother or father, or any other elements of the environment. You will then give the developing fetus the love and comfort it needed but didn't fully receive.

It may happen that you simply feel a sense of calm, peace, and love once you enter the womb. If that's the case, don't try to fix what isn't broken. Take it in and enjoy it.

Take a few deep, letting-go breaths and allow your eyes to close as you begin the process of relaxing both your mind and your body. Relax your feet and legs. Relax your hands and arms. Relax your face, forehead, eyes, and mouth.

Now, take a few moments to observe your thoughts. Just notice what it is you hear your mind saying to you. Now, bring your attention to your heart center, the center of your feelings and emotions. Breathe into your heart, inviting it to open, as this is the doorway to your inner world. As your heart opens, notice the feelings that rise to the surface. Let these feelings come and let them go.

Now, imagine yourself in some place where you feel safe, calm, and relaxed. It can be an actual or imagined place. Use all of your senses as vividly as possible to imagine being there. Get comfortable sitting or lying there and go into a deep meditative state—a state of expanded consciousness. Allow your consciousness to expand beyond the limits of your mental mind. Begin to float, to drift back in time, along the timeline of your life.

Travel back in time now, along that timeline of your life. Go back now to some pleasant or enjoyable occasion very early in childhood, perhaps even baby time. Just let it happen, drift and float all the way back now to something pleasant and enjoyable. Very young. Allow the scene to unfold and trust what comes. It may be something you see, sense, or feel. Just allow the memories to unfold. Notice what is going on around you. Notice how you feel.

Take another deep relaxing breath and continue your journey back in time. Travel back now to that very unique time in the womb, somewhere midway in your development. Move into the womb and your developing body, what are the first things that you notice?

As the caring, loving adult that you are today, reach out to that very little you, hold little you in your hands or put this one into your own womb (if you have one) or into your heart. Hold this very little you and tell them the following: "You are safe, loved, needed, wanted. I see you. Welcome!" Welcome this little you to its developing body, to the family that it's coming to. Welcome this very little you to the world. Give this little you the welcome you needed but didn't get back then. Tell the very little you, "I love you. I am here for you. You are safe with me." As you did with your inner child, ask the very little you what it wants or needs most right now and provide that to the little one.

Feeling safer, more loved, and accepted, begin your journey back to this day and date, time and place. Come all the way back. Reconnect with your body and ground yourself. Breathe deeper again. Move your hands and feet a little. Feel into your hips and pelvis. Open your eyes when you are ready.

The process of reparenting is usually gradual. You don't necessarily need to repeat the practice, but you should connect regularly with the soul you are reparenting for at least a week or more—almost as though you were pregnant with a new life that you need to nourish. This is somewhat parallel to what you did with your inner child. Connecting with your incoming soul is one way to heal early traumas by establishing intimacy and acceptance of who you are at your deepest levels. You may find it helpful to place your hand on your belly and repeat the phrases you used in chapter 4: "I am. I have a right to be. I choose to live."

Perhaps one of the most frequently voiced self-criticisms you must deal with is, "Something is wrong with me." Connecting with and nurturing your soul memories can go a long way toward resolving that self-reproach. And in the process, it moves you toward your ultimate goal of connecting with your soul essence.

CHAPTER 9

Connect with Your Soul Essence and Meet Your Guide

As I hope you now know, deep within each of us dwells a great spirit, a place of profound wisdom, creativity, power, and love that has been obscured by hardened layers of hurt and defenses from early life. Having dug through the layers in the previous chapters, beginning with the conscious interference and heart-opening practices in chapters 1 and 2, you may have already begun to catch glimpses of your soul essence, which is the layer we're focusing on in this chapter.

My first hypnotherapy teacher said that once you move from conscious to subconscious mind and have removed some of the subconscious blocks that are holding you back, you may then begin to progress from subconscious to superconscious mind and to have more profoundly spiritual experiences. At this point in your essential healing journey, you may be starting to notice this too.

Your soul essence carries great wisdom from lifetimes of experience, and it has come to this life with a purpose. It carries an awareness of things it wants to accomplish, valuable lessons it wants to learn in order to grow spiritually. In this chapter, I'll lead you through a variety of methods and give you tools to help you connect with your soul essence and uncover as much of the truth about its mission as you can.

Remember Who You Are and Be That

Sometimes, what we think or believe is our essence is actually an illusion. Dora, a woman in her late twenties, dived through layers to her soul essence only to find a horrible *devil* there, with bulging red, beady eyes. Of course, nobody's soul essence is evil, but this is what she believed was at her core because all through her childhood that's who her father had *told* her she was! If you run into projections that you have adopted or absorbed from others, especially at an early age, you need to know that it is *not* who you are, and you need to keep going. Dora, for instance, kept digging her way through and found a soul essence far more beautiful than she could have imagined, which then expanded outward and broke through all the illusory garbage that her father had laid on her. The process shattered the hurtful image that she had lived with for more than twenty years. It's a powerful process, and because you may need to repeat it a few times to get all the way through, I will offer guidance for reiterating the process.

The following practice replicates and integrates all the previous practices, beginning with the relaxation process from chapter 1. Diving from the mind into the heart, plunging through all the things said and done to us that we have come to believe about ourselves, and exploring all the roles that we've played, we reach into the very core of our being—that place where our soul essence lives. You will make contact with that core self and invite it to come forward. Then you will observe how you feel in its presence. It may have a message, something it wants to show and tell you. Ultimately, you want to invite it to come forward. However you experience your soul essence, your goal is to make contact and bring that inner core self forward.

Just as I have noted that your inner child might sometimes be hiding, you may initially have difficulty locating your soul essence or identifying where it is. As a young girl growing up with a mother who had borderline personality disorder, Adelaide sometimes had a loving mom who was sometimes a scary witch. Not ever knowing which one would appear, she had put her soul essence in a steel container and buried it in the ground to keep it safe. Long after she had grown up and left home, she lost touch with her soul essence and all but forgot where she had hidden it. When Adelaide did this practice and needed to unearth her soul essence, she discovered that it was still ensconced in that steel cylinder that she buried for safekeeping. She opened the container and invited her soul essence out, like the genie being freed from Aladdin's lamp.

If you have trouble locating your soul essence, you should first trust that it's there. You will need to coax it out of hiding by letting it know that it's safe to come forward. You can see or sense what it is like. That's why I often call this process "Remember who you are and be that." You may experience your soul essence as a ball of light, a dancing flame, a glowing crystal, or perhaps as an animal form or bird; you may have auditory or tactile responses, or some combination. You may also experience it as a perception or emotion, something as profound as a feeling that you're a divine being or as simple as a feeling that you're all right after all. Ultimately, your essence is not a mental concept but a state of being.

PRACTICE: Connecting with Your Soul Essence

The goal of this practice is to allow you to dive through the layers you have worked with so far and proceed to your soul essence. The point is not to stop and interact with those layers but primarily to move through them. You may recall some of the work you have done in previous practices, but just observe and keep going toward the soul essence.

Allow your eyes to close and take a few long, slow, deep letting-go breaths, relaxing both mind and body. Begin the process of turning inward and allowing consciousness to expand. Take a few moments to observe your thoughts. Just notice what your mind is saying to you. No need to do anything about it. Just notice what it is saying. And what do you hear it saying?

Now, take some longer, slower, deeper letting-go breaths, shifting your awareness from your thoughts to your feelings. In order to do that, place one hand on the center of your chest, your heart center, and breathe and feel into your heart center, inviting your heart to open. Let those shields, those walls, down, at least for now, and begin your journey inward. Diving deeper and deeper within toward the very core of your being. Like an arrow piercing through the shields, the protections, and the armoring. Diving deeper and deeper within. Toward your core self. Diving past any of the hurts, wounds, or disappointments you may have experienced. Deeper and deeper within. Moving past all the things people said or did to you. Past all of the things that you came to believe of yourself. Diving past all the personas, the different roles you have played. Diving past the mother or father, son or daughter, the partner, husband or wife, brother or sister. Diving past the teacher, the healer, the victim, the pleaser, the responsible one. Keep moving past whatever roles you have adopted. Go deeper and deeper within, toward the very core of your being. Toward that which we call soul essence. Diving through all that you have carried for others, including for your parents, grandparents, and prior generations within your family lineage.

And if you feel more comfortable relaxing your hand at your side at this time, of course that is fine. Go deeper within, past all those crusty layers. For in the very core of your being is your essence, the authentic you. The wise and wonderful you. Your soul essence.

Continue diving deeper within until you can see, feel, and experience before you now that authentic you, your soul essence. In whatever form it might appear, allow yourself to make contact with your essence now. If you have any difficulty in seeing or sensing your soul essence, call to it. Invite it forward or find where it has been hidden for safekeeping and let it out.

Take some time to notice how it feels to be in the presence of this authentic you, this inner wisdom, creativity, power, and love, this soul essence. And your essence has a message for you, something it has wanted to convey to you, perhaps for a long time. Allow yourself to become aware of those words of wisdom, that healing energy or light, whatever it might be. What does the authentic you want to show or tell you?

Let every breath you take be an invocation of your soul essence, calling it forward. Invite it to fill your being—your heart, your mind, and your body. Let it break through those crusty layers that have accumulated over time so it fills you completely. Invite it to grow until it radiates beyond the bounds of your body. (Or, if you prefer, give yourself time to experience your soul essence yourself before sharing it with others.)

Let it fill you and radiate beyond the physical confines of your body and mind. It fills your thoughts, your words, your actions, your home, your life with the essence that has always been there deep within.

And in this more expanded state of awareness, allow yourself to gently and gradually become aware of your surroundings and the new energy in and around you. And gradually open your eyes. Allow yourself to see through these new eyes. Feel through this new skin. Experience the world as your soul essence.

Following this practice, I strongly recommend that you use your journal or a sheet of paper to create an image or series of images, perhaps including words, of how your soul essence appears to you now and what it communicated to you during the practice. For that reason, you can creatively combine images and words if that feels appropriate. Then you can leave the paper out in your home, office, or bedroom. This isn't about artistic skill but about creating a cue to help recall the experience—again, to remember who you truly are. It's a good idea to look occasionally at what you've written and at your drawing in the days following your soul essence practice. I encourage you to pay attention to how you now look at other people, whether they are loved ones whom you see every day or people you encounter by chance in a store or restaurant.

For days after my own soul essence breakthrough, I lived and breathed the experience. As time went on, perhaps inevitably, the power of the experience faded somewhat, and I learned that I had to continue to nurture and facilitate the emergence of my soul essence. Indeed, I would say that you can expect this falling off of intensity, which even many highly realized spiritual practitioners and teachers have experienced.[20]

Once you've done the practice to completion, you should find it easier and quicker to repeat it as a way of nurturing your connection with your soul essence. The more you do this, by checking in with your soul essence, moving into your heart, and then engaging your mental mind from that perspective, the more natural it will seem. Over time, this could become a regular, even daily, practice.

Certainly, it is necessary to look deep inside before you can reach for higher levels of awareness. It has been said by spiritual teachers of many traditions that we all have within us a spark of the divine, or Buddha nature, and that we only have to clear away the obscurations with which we have covered it over.

Now that you've connected with your soul essence, you can begin to move further forward along your path. After gaining access to your own internal wisdom, you can go beyond that and reach out to your higher wisdom. You have already resolved issues in your body and in your subconscious en route to contacting your core. As enlightened as your own soul essence is in comparison to your conscious mind, your soul carries with it other issues that you need to resolve, as we saw in the previous chapter. One approach to identifying and resolving those issues is to connect with your guide to help you review your progress in this life.

Guides Are Loving Teachers

One of the most profound aspects of my near-death experience was that even as my body seemed to have died, my consciousness continued to function. It persisted independently of my mental mind and body and well beyond the normal constraints of time and space. And something else was made plain to me. I realized that, contrary to my worst fears, I was not alone. I had help in all this. The part of me that could look down on my body, which had been struck by lightning, continued to move away from the earth, went on to meet my guide, and had an experience of complete and unconditional love.

This is what was happening, as I described in the introduction, when my fellow hypnotherapist David Quigley led me through a regression back to my near-death experience. I suddenly received input from a wise and loving being of whom I had been largely unaware. That being ushered me in to the "Universal Sea of Consciousness," where I felt connected with all life and yet maintained my sense of self—albeit without the feeling of separation that usually accompanies self-awareness. During that extraordinary experience, a message came to me. "Listen," it said. "Listen to spirit. You have a wonderful mind, but you rely on it far too much. Meditate, turn inward, and listen. Spirit speaks to you constantly; all you need to do is listen. Listen to your heart. Listen to your soul. Listen to spirit."

I further received a message that the work I was doing was "on the right path" but that I needed to approach the work with more heart and soul rather than mere intellectual understanding. At the time, it was clear to me that this was not the inner voice of my higher self or soul essence but was coming from my guide. I was aware of the concept of spiritual guides from having read Raymond Moody and Michael Newton but had never sensed having a relationship with a guide as a being separate from me. As I've said, I didn't "hear" an auditory voice in my head, but I did feel as if I were receiving a thought-stream from some external source.

Most of us have more than one guide. People who practice mediumship often rely on more than one guide to deliver information from "the other side," and those guides are often distinct from their primary guide.

Suzanne Giesemann, a former Navy commander and a leading teacher of mediumship, acknowledges that some guides have a specific role or function, but that we all have "at least one main spirit guide, who is with you from your first earthly breath until your last."[21] Of course, that same guide has also been with you in previous lifetimes and will be with you in the future. Reporting what her own guides have said to her, Giesemann relays their message:

> All of us are here to answer your questions and provide assistance, and yet we will not answer those questions that require you to learn through your own effort and choices. We will answer you in the best way that we can, be that through intuitive nudges, be that by bringing just the right person into your life, be that by impressing thoughts upon your consciousness.[22]

Guides always advocate for free will, and they rarely if ever tell us to do something. They want us to learn and so are as likely to ask us questions as to answer ours. But they communicate in a variety of ways, as we will see, and you should be alert to the different forms that their communications might assume.

"I'm Here with You"

Ruby was about fifty when she did the "Meet Your Guide and Review Your Life" practice, which you'll do later in this chapter. Her reason for seeking help was the feeling that she had no one to support her during most of her life. She felt alone and unsupported by her parents, her partner, or her coworkers. When she hoped to meet her guide during the practice and, *Surprise!*, there was no guide, she took this as confirmation that she really was *not* supported by anyone. In my experience, however, everyone has a guide—or, more likely, several guides—and it's just a matter of making contact.

As Ruby was becoming increasingly irritated, she realized that far in the distance she did sense a presence of some kind and wondered if that might be her guide. In most cases, your guide will come forward to meet you or you will feel yourself drawn toward them. But sometimes, especially if you're feeling a strong resistance, they may hang back a bit. In her impatience, Ruby started to complain. "Why aren't you here?" she asked almost bitterly. "Why aren't you helping me?"

In that moment, the guide moved closer to her. She didn't describe his appearance, but she did use the male pronoun. He waved his hand and pointed to a scene from her most recent past life. In that life, which had ended rather early, she saw that she had not accomplished much, for which she felt deep regret. Upon exiting that life, Ruby formed the soul intention to work much harder and prove that she could be successful all on her own. The guide said, "You expressed that you wanted to live this life on your own. But it doesn't have to be that way. I can help you, but only if you ask."

Because Ruby made a contract to do it all by herself, her promise remained strongly impressed in her consciousness. Her guide couldn't simply wave a magic wand and change her decision. It would take time, and she would have to turn the page, as it were, see the futility of her prior contract, and agree to let her guide help her. She gradually understood that her guide had always been there and only needed her to ask for his assistance. He embraced her and repeated that she was not alone. "I'm here with you," he said, "and I always have been."

Guides are always teaching us, as much in how they appear and interact with us as in what they tell us. They don't need to say they love you; their very presence often fills you with a radiant feeling of being loved.

Guides Help Us Learn and Grow

That feeling of being loved unconditionally is another of the gifts that guides provide. In the numerous published accounts of near-death experiences, the first thing many people mention is their encounter with a "being of light." Although people having a near-death experience may also mention being greeted by deceased loved ones, they generally recount the awe-filled experience of being welcomed by a bright light radiating warmth and unconditional love unlike anything they have experienced on Earth. This being of light is usually a spirit guide whose role is to calm any fear and anxiety on the part of the person having the near-death experience. The guide is often the one who informs them that they must return to life on Earth. In some cases, they offer the option to return to life or to continue and cross the threshold to "the other side," which would amount to dying physically—although that is reported less often than the simple command that they must return because they have more to learn or accomplish.

Michael Newton's contribution to the field of regression was to guide his clients under deep hypnosis to explore an extended sojourn in the period between their death in a previous life and their rebirth into their current life. What they went through was similar in many ways to a near-death experience, particularly their discovery that they had a primary guide who had been with them through many lives. But they also reported interactions with other guides and wise beings who helped them with different aspects of their lives.

One of the most comforting and gratifying experiences of working with regression has been getting to meet not only my own guides but also those of the numerous people I have helped to connect with these astonishing beings. More highly evolved souls than most human beings, our spirit guides have been with us for eons, but many of us are still unaware that we have guides, and even less so of how to connect with them and how much they can help us. Guides are there to help us learn and grow, not to criticize, punish, or belittle us.

Many people describe their initial encounter with their guide as like meeting up with a long-lost friend. You may feel as if something that has been missing from your life has finally been reestablished and that you feel fully understood as if for the first time. If your guide initially behaves otherwise, it's a signal that they are role-playing for a reason. If your guide acts like a comic, as mine once did, it may be trying to tell you to lighten up. When they seem to be carping, they may be mirroring your own hypercritical attitude toward yourself or others.

You Have All the Answers Within You

Guides often communicate through images, as well as their behavior. Invited to write down a few questions for her guide, Maria prepared four single-spaced pages encompassing a laundry list of metaphysical inquiries. When she did the practice and met her guide, her first question was, "How are souls created?" Her guide seemed to shrug his shoulders. She didn't understand what he meant and repeated the question. "I don't know," he said. "You tell me." Guides can be humorous at times, but this one was trying to send a message. When she followed with a similar question, he finally said, "You've been to every kind of psychic, tarot reader, astrologer, and medium, asking them these same kinds of questions. You have to understand that you have within you all the wisdom you need."

To further make his point, Maria's guide showed her what she described as a vast structure that resembled an ancient library, with endless rows of bookshelves on many levels. The message was that she needed to learn to rely on her own internal resources.

At other times, guides can be surprisingly specific. An artist I knew once asked her guide to help her find a place she could stay in New York City that would be affordable but spacious enough to do her painting. She had been living for many years at the Chelsea Hotel, the residence on Twenty-Third Street in Manhattan, which was once home to legendary artists, writers, and musicians, from Dylan Thomas to Sid Vicious. But the hotel had changed hands, the new owner was renovating it, and rents were skyrocketing, so she had to move out. Her guide showed her what looked like Google Maps with an arrow pointing to the corner of a street on the west side of Midtown Manhattan. She said the location seemed unlikely because it was in the middle of a commercial district, but when she went there, she found a residential loft for rent in her price range and large enough for her to paint in.

What You Need to Know Before Meeting Your Guide

Although your primary guide has been with you all your life, you may not be aware of their presence. In that sense, your meeting is a kind of reunion. Your guide likely has their own plan of what and how they want to communicate with you. So, along with asking your questions, be sure to spend time just listening to what your guide has to share with you. Their communications are about more than the simple transfer of information; they want to give your soul an experience beyond the cognitive level that may evoke awe and other emotions. For instance, you might ask your guide to give you an experience of unconditional love or of oneness.

There is an energetic aspect to communicating with your guide, so take that in as well. Above all, be open and absorptive, taking it in from the depths of your being. Listen from your heart and soul, not merely from your mind.

Be aware that your guide may or may not have a human form, let alone a specific gender, and is just as likely to be a shapeless ball of light or even something nonvisual—a warm, loving energy. They appear however they choose, and how they appear can be significant. Guides communicate telepathically, so you shouldn't expect to see them talking or moving their lips. You may "hear" their communications in your inner mind. They converse in metaphor and are likely to show you visual symbols or images, but they may also lead you through certain experiences to get their point across. People often report being shown a past life by their guide or finding themselves in the middle of the life itself, an experience some have likened to virtual reality. The parallel to VR is helpful because when you are having a virtual reality experience, you know it isn't happening on a physical plane, and yet it feels like you are right there in the midst of things.

If you are asking your guide a question silently, you may get a response in your mind but may wonder if you just made it up. That can happen, but when you are trying to formulate your question and you get an answer before you ask the question, that's a good sign that you've established a solid connection. Remember, your guide may communicate to you through telepathic messages, metaphor, images, experiences, and feelings.

What We Carry Over

Besides the stored emotions and limiting beliefs that we carry in our subconscious, we also carry beliefs in our soul from previous lifetimes. One important reason we are here on Earth is to understand the source of these limiting beliefs and to overcome them.

A life review is often part of a near-death experience. In the next practice, you're going to facilitate your own life review with your guide without having to almost die. This is the stage where you may be able to resolve some of the limiting misunderstandings carried over from previous soul experiences. I first encountered the idea that our souls agree in advance to work on learning certain lessons over the course of lifetimes from Henry Leo Bolduc, who wrote *Life Patterns, Soul Lessons, and Forgiveness*. For Bolduc, the main reason we live more than one life is to learn a series of lessons.[23]

As I mentioned in chapter 3, during my childhood I suffered such a severe case of arthritis that at age four, I had to stay in a convalescent home in Northern California. I was in a wheelchair and had to be fed and bathed by the staff. Through intensive physical therapy and a series of steroid injections, I was cured of the arthritis within a year or so, and remarkably have no trace of that ailment today. Years later, during a guide session, my guide showed me several prior lifetimes in which I devoted myself to caretaking others and neglecting myself. I was apparently planning to repeat that theme in this life, but I discovered that, as my life began, I was completely disabled so I would be unable to care for myself and would have to learn to let others care for me—to receive instead of always giving. That may sound like a harsh way to learn a lesson, although I'm sure it was harder on my parents. Even though I was able to see my need to learn to let myself be taken care of, the momentum of past lives was impelling my soul to repeat the caregiver pattern. I still tend to be a caregiver for others, and I'm certain that if I hadn't gone through that early childhood ailment, I might well have repeated that pattern yet again.

PRACTICE: Meet Your Guide and Review Your Life

In this practice, you will become aware of your guide's presence; you will reunite with your guide and begin communicating directly with them. After your reunion, you can ask them to review your current life and soul lessons with you. You may want to write out a few questions in advance. It's best to keep them short and simple and limit them to two or three things that concern you personally.

If you're unclear about something the guide is showing you, it's fine to ask directly. Check if they are intending what you believe they are. A guide might show you a ladder going to heaven, and it could mean it's time to go somewhere, but it could also symbolize climbing a ladder to go to a higher plane of awareness to communicate with your guide. You can ask your guide which interpretation is most relevant. You may wonder why they don't just tell you something in so many words. If you want to know why they do that, ask them when you're there. If you're having trouble understanding, tell them that and ask for more clarity.

This practice has two sections: reunion and life review. You can also adapt this practice to ask specific questions of your guide without having to do your life review again. In the reunion section, take time to reconnect with your guide, feeling their love and support and being open to what your guide wants to communicate to you. In the life review section, you will have the opportunity to ask your guide about your purpose and soul lessons.

Before finishing the practice, ask your guide how you can connect with them more directly on your own. They may suggest that you engage in meditation, automatic writing, walks in nature, or other modes that are readily available to almost anyone.

Allow your eyes to close and take a few long, slow, deep letting-go breaths, relaxing both mind and body. Begin the process of turning inward and allowing consciousness to expand. Take a few moments to observe your thoughts. Notice what your mind is saying to you.

Now, take some longer, slower, deeper letting-go breaths and shift your awareness from your thoughts to your feelings. To do that, place one hand on the center of your chest, your heart center, and breathe and feel into your heart, inviting your heart to open, and begin your journey inward. Diving deeper and deeper within, toward the very core of your being, going directly to your soul essence. Make contact with your soul essence now and become one with it, allowing your consciousness to expand even further.

In this highest state of expanded consciousness, turn toward your guide or become aware of your guide's presence. See, feel, or experience your guide right there with you now.

Reunion. Notice how your guide appears. Notice how it feels to be in your guide's presence. Be open now to what your guide wants to communicate to you. Listen from the depths of your being, your soul essence. What does your guide show you or tell you? Be open and receptive to what your guide offers you.

Life review. Ask your guide to help you review your life. You can ask what your soul's purpose is, what you are here to do, and what you are here to learn. You can also ask whether you have contracts to meet specific people, including a soul mate. Ask how you're doing with your lessons, that is, how you are progressing. You might ask what beliefs and survival strategies you have carried over from previous lives and how they are affecting you.

When you are finished with your questions, ask your guide how you can stay in touch and thank the guide for its assistance before returning to your normal state of consciousness. If you feel it would be helpful, you can ask your guide for a name by which you can call it. (Most guides will say they don't use names, recognizing each other by the nature of their light or sound vibration, but that they understand our need for names.)

Remaining connected with your guide and your soul essence, come all the way back now. Feel into your body. Become aware of your room or surroundings, grounding and connecting yourself. When you're ready, open your eyes.

Take a few moments to write or record the insights you have gained while meeting and communicating with your guide. The more often you reach out to your guide, the easier it becomes to establish lines of communication. In time, you can simply turn inward to call on your guide, ask a question, and get your answer on the spot without going through a preamble. Not only will you find it easier to make the connection without first doing a long practice, but you will also need to rely less on your literal mind and more on your intuitive instincts. You begin to communicate on a higher level of consciousness; you will do less thinking and worrying and more intuiting and sensing. We like to have things spelled out and often rely too much on what our mind thinks we want. But you're more likely to end up with what you really want if you begin by checking in with your intuition, and then using your mind's logic and reason to put your intuitive instinct and inner messages into action.

You Can Ask Your Guide Specific Questions

After doing your life review, you can easily adapt the practice to meet and consult with your guide about specific questions on which you need guidance, without having to do a life review. Some time ago, I was trying to decide whether to leave a nonprofit for which I'd been working for fifteen years. It had been a positive experience, but I was beginning to have second thoughts about many of their rules and regulations. When I let the organization know I was thinking of leaving, they countered by offering me an attractive promotion. I could move into the headquarters and be named as an administrator and vice-president, and learned that they would be grooming me to become the next president. It was an appealing offer, and I talked it over with a friend, a therapist, and my guide. My guide, not wanting to tell me what to do, summed it up for me this way: "Help me understand," he said, using classic therapeutic lingo. "You're having difficulties with the rules and regulations of this organization. And you're going to become the administrator and enforce those rules and regulations on everyone else?" That was more effective than if my guide had insisted I not take the offer.

When you want to connect with your guide, first take a few moments to connect with your soul essence. From that state of expanded consciousness, connect with your guide as you've been doing. Tell your guide that you've come to visit today because you need their help with something.

You now have a series of processes for self-healing that you can continue to practice on your own. As I discovered in my early work as a clinical hypnotherapist, anesthetizing pain is only a symptomatic approach—working from the outside in, as it were. True healing means going deeper within, locating the source of the pain and healing from the inside out. Connecting with the soul essence that has been buried deep inside you makes that possible. As that essence emerges, breaking through and sloughing off crusty layers of old beliefs, protections, and stored emotions, you begin to live from the inside out on a regular basis. Instead of treating only the symptoms, you reach in deeper to the root of the pain.

The core idea behind essential healing is to gain access to wisdom that ranges beyond your intellect, your life experience, and even your heart. The heart is the doorway, not the destination. Your soul essence may not yet be fully perfected, but it's far more developed than your mind or heart. Connecting with it opens the pathway to a more authentic and satisfying way of living. You now have the tools to help you be that authentic you and, with it, to embody a new way of life.

Practice Guide

Here is a practical guide for applying some of the self-healing processes that you have been working with.

Condition	Practice
Pain, Illness	Accessing the Body Wisdom Process, chapter 7
Sleep difficulty	Reminding Your Body "I Am Safe," Finding Your Safe Place, chapter 1 Redirecting Your Part, chapter 5
Anxiety/fear	Going out of your mind Reminding Your Body "I Am Safe," Resetting the Protective Alert Level of Your "Control Room," chapter 1
Worry/confusion, crossroads	Awakening the Wise Woman Within; Awakening the Wise Man Within, chapter 7 Meet Your Guide and Review Your Life, chapter 9
Loss (death, health, employment, finances, freedom, way of life)	Redirecting Your Part, chapter 5

Condition	Practice
Depression	The Volcano Release, The Balloon Release, Releasing Your Burden, chapter 3 Redirecting Your Part, chapter 5
Anger	The Volcano Release, The Balloon Release, Releasing Your Burden, chapter 3 Redirecting Your Part, chapter 5
Trauma retriggered	Reminding Your Body "I Am Safe," Finding Your Safe Place, chapter 1 Redirecting Your Part, chapter 5

Acknowledgments

Sophia, my everything. My wife, best friend, sounding board, critic, partner, cheerleader, editor, inspiration, listener. You saw something in me that I didn't see and with such love and acceptance helped me grow into who I am today. Thank you for all your love, support, space to write, encouragement, patience, and occasional push to keep me going and make sure this got written.

Peter Occhiogrosso, you heard my voice and helped me share it on these pages. Thank you for the many creative hours spent discussing the meaning of a word, researching topics, and developing concepts so I could convey them clearly and meaningfully. I truly admire you for your brilliant intellect, sly humor, depth of experience, and artful guidance that made this book possible.

Leslie Meredith, my agent, thank you for believing in me. I am grateful for how you advocated for me and skillfully guided me through every step of this new journey as an author. Your keen eye and extensive editorial experience were unexpected contributions that I deeply appreciate.

Many thanks to my editors, Ryan Buresh and Jennifer Holder, and the team at New Harbinger for daring to be different by developing a writing and publishing process that supports working authors like me, so I could continue teaching and doing sessions while writing. You challenged me, you encouraged me, and your editorial work was masterful. Thank you for bringing out the best in this book.

Michael Newton, my dear friend and brilliant mentor, who challenged and inspired me in so many ways that I will always be grateful for. I am so glad that we met and shared our passion for bodysurfing after those long, intense days of training in Virginia Beach and that those special moments led to a deep friendship and our working and teaching together.

Henry Leo Bolduc, thank you for being the first to encourage me to write and to offer me mentoring as I was beginning my career as a therapist.

My friend Tom Nolan, thank you for hounding me about getting this book written. Your gentle persistence kept me going!

Endnotes

1   Maia Davis, "Lightning Victims Scarred by Ordeal," *The Record* (July 21, 1998).

2   Jack Williams, "How Lightning Kills and Injures Victims," *Washington Post* (June 27, 2013), https://www.washingtonpost.com /news/capital-weather-gang/wp/2013/06/27/how-lightning-kills -and-injures-victims/.

3   Caroline Myss, *Sacred Contracts: Awakening Your Divine Potential* (New York: Harmony Books, 2001), 373.

4   For more on the wonder child, see Emmet Fox, *The Wonder Child* (Camarillo, CA: Devorss & Co., 1932).

5   Ellen Bass and Laura Davis, *The Courage to Heal: A Guide for Women Survivors of Child Sexual Abuse*, revised, expanded edition (New York: William Morrow, 2008).

6   Jonathan Mayne, ed., *Charles Baudelaire, The Painter of Modern Life,* (United Kingdom: Phaidon Publishers, 1970) see essay titled "An Artist, Man of the World, Man of Crowds, and Child."

7   Although my approach to parts therapy is tailored to the way I use it in my healing workshops, I can recommend three books on the subject by authors I admire. David Quigley, *Alchemical Hypnosis: A Manual of Practical Technique* (CreateSpace, 2016, originally published in 1984). Roy Hunter, *Hypnosis for Inner Conflict Resolution: Introducing Parts Therapy* (Crown House Publishing, Ltd., 2005). Charles Tebbetts, *Self-Hypnosis and Other Mind Expanding Techniques* (Port Saint Lucie, FL: Westwood Publishing, 1977).

8   Flora Rheta Schreiber, *Sybil: The Classic True Story of a Woman Possessed by Sixteen Separate Personalities* (New York: Grand Central Publishing, 1973).

9   Carl Jung, *The Archetypes and the Collective Unconscious* (Princeton, NJ: Princeton University Press, 1968), 284.

10 Richard A. Cordell, *Somerset Maugham: A Biographical and Critical Study* (Bloomington: Indiana University Press, 1961) includes a discussion of this quotation. The biographer contends that Maugham's comment was inspired by his exposure to the Maxims of La Rochefoucauld in his youth.

11 Sophia Kramer is a certified master hypnotherapist and instructor specializing in family systems, past life and Life Between Lives regression therapy and spiritual healing. Her passion is to help people understand their soul's journey and reintegrate their fragmented soul parts.

12 Bridgitte Jackson-Buckley, "What Is Soul Retrieval?" Gaia (March 30, 2017), https://www.gaia.com/article/what-is-soul -retrieval. Sandra Ingerman, *Soul Retrieval: Mending the Fragmented Self* (New York: HarperOne, 2006).

13 Henry Maudsley, *The Physiology and Pathology of Mind* (New York: D. Appleton & Comp, 1874), 138.

14 See especially Peggy Huddleston, *Prepare for Surgery, Heal Faster: A Guide of Mind-Body Techniques*, 4th ed. (New York: Angel River, 2012).

15 Michael Newton, *Journey of Souls: Case Studies of Life Between Lives* (Portland, OR: Llewellyn Worldwide, 1994), 3–4.

16 Newton, *Journey*, 3.

17 Moheb Costandi, "Where Are Old Memories Stored in the Brain?" *Scientific American* (February 10, 2009), https://www.scientific american.com/article/the-memory-trace/.

18 Bruce H. Lipton, *The Biology of Belief: Unleashing the Power of Consciousness, Matter & Miracles*, revised edition (Carlsbad: Hay House, 2015), 122, 179–180. See also Thomas R. Verny and Pamela Weintraub, *Pre-Parenting: Nurturing Your Child from Conception* (New York: Simon & Schuster, 2003).

19 Newton, *Journey*, 266–267.

20 The esteemed American Buddhist teacher Jack Kornfield filled an entire book with stories of experienced meditation teachers and practitioners from several spiritual traditions who, after achieving high levels of realization, still faced the task of translating that freedom into everyday life—not always successfully. See Kornfield, *After the Ecstasy, the Laundry: How the Heart Grows Wise on the Spiritual Path* (New York: Bantam, 2001).

21 Suzanne Giesemann, *Mediumship: Working with your Guides*, audio CD (Hemi-Sync, 2018).

22 Giesemann, *Mediumship*.

23 Henry Leo Bolduc, *Life Patterns, Soul Lessons, and Forgiveness* (New York: Adventures into Time, 1994).

Based in New York, NY, **Paul Aurand** is an award-winning master hypnotherapist who has worked in the field for more than thirty years. He survived being struck by lightning and had a transformative near-death experience (NDE) that he has integrated into his Essential Healing workshops, which he presents internationally. Aurand served as the first elected president of the Michael Newton Institute, and now serves as its director of education and lead trainer. He has been featured in documentary films and on television for his work with the groundbreaking Life Between Lives regression therapy.

MORE BOOKS for the SPIRITUAL SEEKER

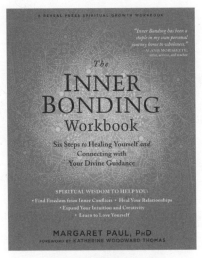
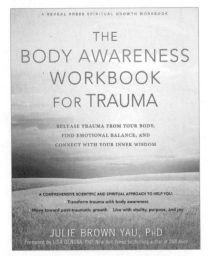
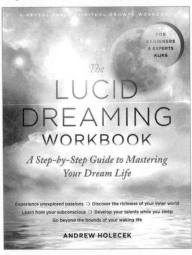
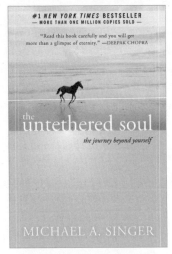